BRITISH MUSLIM EXPECTATIONS OF THE GOVERNMENT

THE BRITISH MEDIA AND MUSLIM REPRESENTATION: THE IDEOLOGY OF DEMONISATION

SAIED R. AMELI
SYED MOHAMMED MARANDI
SAMEERA AHMED
SEYFEDDIN KARA
AND ARZU MERALI

2007
PUBLISHED BY ISLAMIC HUMAN RIGHTS COMMISSION

First published in Great Britain in 2007
by Islamic Human Rights Commission
PO Box 598, Wembley, HA9 7XH

© 2007 Islamic Human Rights Commission

Printed in England by Islamic Human Rights Commission
Design & Typeset: Ibrahim Sadikovic
Printed by Impeks Print

All rights reserved. No part of this book may be reprinted or reproduced or utilised in any form or by any means electronic, mechanical, or other means, now known or hereinafter invented, including photocopying and recording, or in any information storage or retrieval system, without permission in writing from the publishers.

ISBN 1-903718-31-7

CONTENTS

- Acknowledgments 6
- Foreword 7
- Introduction 8
- Background Studies 10
  - Representation of Muslims in British Media 10
  - Basic Theory and Concept of Representation 10
  - Muslim Perception of the Media 13
  - Domination, Demonisation or Both? The 'Common Sense' of Television News and Cinema 19
  - Otherness, the Orient, Islam and Muslims: Understanding the Role and Effect of Literature and Cinema on Society and Social Actors 22
- Methodology and Sample Group 25
- Research Findings 26

PART ONE: Textual Analysis – Representation of Muslims in British Media Text 26
- Representation of Muslims in British Television News 26
  - Asylum and Immigration 28
  - Loyalty and Belonging 29
  - Global Dimensions and Geopolitics 31
- The Big Screen - Muslim Representation in Cinema 34
  - Arab and Islam as a Symbol of Violence 39
  - Racism, Islamophobia or Both? 41
- The Rule of the Occident in English Literature 47
  - Beyond Occident / Orient 58

PART TWO: Contextual Analysis – British Muslims' Understanding of Muslim Representation in the Media 59
  - Age Groups and Perception of Media 61
  - Gender and Perception of Media 61
  - Birthplace and Perception of Media 62
  - Level of Religiosity and Perception of Media 64
  - Education and the Perception of Media 65
  - Representation of Muslims in the British Media 67
  - Portrayal of British Muslims and Non-British Muslims 70
  - Islamophobia in Hollywood and British Movies 72
  - Different Representations in the Different Forms of Media ... 74
  - Complaints and Responses 77
  - Ideological Representation: Encoded Messages about Muslims 78
  - Phobic Representation of Muslims: Intercultural Consequences 80
  - Impacts on Non-Muslims 82
  - Responsibility of Media regarding Islamophobia 83
  - Does the Media Give Enough Opportunity to Muslims? 87
  - Muslim Expectations from the Media 89
- Comment from Community Figures and Academics 92
- Concluding Remarks 98
- Recommendations 100
- Bibliography 104
- Appendices 110

LIST OF FIGURES AND TABLES

Figure 1:	What are your Feelings on the Portrayal of Muslims and Islam in the British Media?	67
Table 1:	Articles containing the Word 'Muslim'	15
Table 2:	Frequently Occurring Words	27
Table 3:	Terror and Global Dimensions	31
Table 4:	Al-Qaeda and Osama bin Laden	32
Table 5:	Location and Perception of Media	60
Table 6:	Age Group and Perception of Media	61
Table 7:	Gender and Perception of Media	62
Table 8:	Place of Birth and Perception of Media	63
Table 9:	Citizenship status and Perception of Media	63
Table 10:	Affiliation and Perception of Media	64
Table 11:	Level of Religiosity and Perception of Media	65
Table 12:	Educational level and Perception of Media	66
Table 13:	Discrimination and Perception of Media	86
Table 14:	Representation and Perception of Media	89

APPENDICES

Investigative Framework

Table (i)	TV News Analysis – BBC News – Politics and Security issues	110
Table (ii)	TV News Analysis – BBC News – Social and Cultural Descriptions	111
Table (iii)	TV News Analysis – Newsnight – Politics and Security issues	112
Table (iv)	TV News Analysis – Newsnight – Social and Cultural Descriptions	113
Table (v)	TV News Analysis – ITV News – Politics and Security issues	114
Table (vi)	TV News Analysis – ITV News – Social and Cultural Descriptions	115
Table (vii)	TV News Analysis – Channel 4 – Politics and Security issues	116
Table (viii)	TV News Analysis – Channel 4 – Social and Cultural Descriptions	117

ACKNOWLEDGMENTS

IHRC would like to acknowledge the Joseph Rowntree Charitable Trust for their support for this project.

Thanks also to the following for their commitment and dedication to this volume and this series: Aisha Abbasi, Hiba Abdul Rahim, Faaria Ahmad, Musthak Ahmed, Gloria Amadi, Fahad Ansari, Beena Faridi, Huda Hlaiyil, Karin Lindahl, Zeeya Merali, Abidah Merchant, Abbas Nawrozzadeh, Humza Qureshi, Zainab Shadjareh and Ahmed Uddin.

The following also provided insight into the various issues covered in this volume: Faisal Bodi, Arun Kundnani, Nasfim Haque, Anthony Mcroy, Ismail Adam Patel, Emdad Rahman and Yvonne Ridley.

Particular thanks also to Dr. Peter de Bolla, Dr. Steve Hewitt, Anjie Sandhu and Professor Jan Aart Scholte for their suggestions and critical insight.

We also wish to acknowledge Saloomeh, Seyed Mohammad Sadegh, Seyed Mohammad Sajjad, Senar Madali Muhammed Hadi Ailan and a special thanks to Nuru-l-Huda, for helping out wherever she could.

FOREWORD

At the time of writing up this report Lebanon was burning and Gaza was under siege. Pictures of war crimes, collective punishment, mass bombings and mass burials pervaded our TV screens. How does this relate to the representation of Muslims in the British media, and why should a 'foreign' war be so important to the ideas that pertain to this volume, namely the relationship between effective citizenship for (Muslim) minorities, and their representation in the media, specifically literature, cinema, and TV news?

As this war was fought, a battle over terminology was and is being ferociously waged on a daily basis, with British political language at odds with the representations on the screen: the government talks about Hizbullah aggression while TV screens show Israeli war crimes; the government talks about ending external interference in Lebanon and Gaza from Iran and Syria, and news bulletins show an Israeli onslaught on both besieged nations. A war between civil society and pro-Israeli elements rages in the press, and the government has fallen into line with a societal reading of Islam and Muslims, wherever they are, as aggressive and aggressors, despite overwhelming evidence to the contrary such as in Lebanon and Gaza. The view is of Muslims as incorrigibly savage and beyond negotiations. Peace will come on Israeli, US and British terms, not those dictated by Muslims, or indeed, international law.

This polarisation of representations highlights the core of this volume's aim – to dissect how cultural and social policy is informed by media representation of Muslims – which as current events have shown is not always intentionally inimical – but which nevertheless has a huge part to play in shaping negative perception of Muslims and creating negative experiences for Muslims at individual and collective levels.

By decoding cultural narratives in literature and film and analysing TV news reporting in the UK about Muslims after the bombings of July 7, 2005, this volume explores the relationship between perceptions by and of Muslims and the role of domination and demonisation in the cultural language of media and power. Without understanding how power is structured through convention and how this necessarily excludes and mutes minorities' demands, we cannot begin to move beyond a cycle of suspicion and segregation enforced by powerful majority cultural expectations.

As so many 'others' die, it is incumbent on all those who seek a truly cohesive and just society for tomorrow to understand how these deaths and the language that cheapens them results from a discourse of demonisation that exists here, and now, and in this country.

Islamic Human Rights Commission

INTRODUCTION

The media today occupies a pivotal position in society and its ubiquitous presence signifies the enormous potential it has for informing people about everyday issues. The media is seen not only as transferring information and ideas but also as shaping opinions and presenting particular versions of reality (Gurevitch, *et al*, 1995). Though different media forms, ranging from traditional press to new electronic sources, are qualitatively different from one another, their overall impact is evident through their widespread presence and the reliance placed on them as authentic purveyors of news and information. Furthermore, the media holds a central position in articulating particular discourses and defining frameworks within which we come to understand issues relating to minority groups (Cottle, 2000).

Media representation of minorities and minority group issues – or indeed the lack of representation – is a key factor in determining how majority audiences think about minorities in their societies. Whilst on the one hand media creates the 'invisibility of minorities' by marginalising their voices, on the other, actual portrayals more often than not fall into restricted and negatively stereotyped contexts (Campbell, 1995). An important aspect of Campbell's work, echoed by others, is that the "dangerous ignorance about people of colour and a continuance of discrimination and injustice" is not unconnected with their treatment in the media (p. 7). Similarly van Dijk (2000) states that media discourse is the main source of people's knowledge, attitudes and ideologies. When this discourse is specifically about minority groups and additionally the audience has limited 'contact' with these groups, the role of media as the sole provider of information becomes even more critical.

These ideas can be directly applied to media coverage of Muslim minorities living in the West as well as the worldwide Muslim community. Whilst racist discourse has been identified in relation to ethnic minorities, this racial prejudice is supplemented by anti-Islamic rhetoric in almost all Western media when it comes to presenting issues linked to Islam and Muslims (Henzell-Thomas, 2001). It can be argued that religion *per se* suffers at the hands of media, but it is recognised that the media seem to have a distinct aversion to Islam and Muslims (Said, 1996).

For some time now Muslims in Britain, and across the Western world, have expressed their concerns about the way Islam is portrayed in the media. Aside from the actual inaccuracies and negativity prevalent in media discourse, they feel that people's perceptions of their faith and beliefs are adversely affected by such representation. The link between media representation and public perception in this context has been examined through various studies and polls and is an area of concern for the general public, community organisations and government bodies (IQRA Trust/MORI, 1990, Mian, 1997 and Poole, 2001). In promoting harmony between different groups in society, the government may well need to influence the function of media in developing understanding and mutual tolerance and respect, whilst at the same time acknowledging its right to independent reporting. Voluntary codes and guidelines may not be sufficient in eliminating the prejudicial portrayals in the media and firmer steps, perhaps leading to legislation, may be a more effective means through which to ensure media take greater responsibility in their role as contributors to public knowledge.

Numerous critiques have been made of coverage of issues relating to Islam and Muslims following September 2001[1]. The purpose of this research is to re-examine the situation of these media discourses using three genres: television news, mainstream cinema and canonical and popular English literature.

In doing so not only is the study identifying how the media places Islam and British Muslims (and Muslims in general) within a certain frame of reference, but it is also examining the potential media have of changing these reference points. Can British Muslim communities be deconstructed from their position as the 'other' or the 'enemy within', and be projected as fellow citizens within a multi-ethnic and multi-religious society in which all belief systems are respected equally? If concepts of citizenship – involving responsibilities as well as rights – are to be valued equally by all members of society, then it is only correct that their representation in the media should reflect this.

The specific issue for this research then is to identify the language and discourse relating to Islam and Muslims that is prevalent in television news programmes, literature (both classic and popular) and mainstream cinema films. The reasons these types of media have been selected will be discussed below. The questions being asked in this study are:

- How has the Western media generally covered Islam and Muslims?
- What are the prevailing discourses about Islam and Muslims that can be identified in selected forms of media?
- What are the concerns about media reporting and why does representation matter?
- What action can Muslims expect the government to take to remedy any unfairness?

Ultimately, the objective of analysing 'representation' is to understand how it can influence public understanding and viewpoints. Through the subtle (and sometimes blatant) propagation of the hegemonic ideological stance, the media can influence and adapt our ideas about one group in society and this in turn can impact on their position through prejudice, discrimination and marginalisation. The ability of powerful groups to 'represent' others in certain, stereotypical ways, emphasising their difference, is what Hall (1997) defines as *symbolic* power – the power to mark, assign and classify. By not employing older forms of vulgar, biological racist discourses, the 'new' racisms are more insidious in their nature, depicting minorities as inferior through their 'differences' – 'they' are different because they have a different culture and different values from 'us' (Mistry, 1999).

These 'common sense' notions about race and minority groups are gradually normalised and the media continues to reinforce them by confining debate to a set of narrow thematic structures. In talking about the 'discursive reproduction of racism', van Dijk (2000) observes that, "the beliefs and 'social representation' many members of the dominant (white) in-group have about immigrants and minorities are largely derived from discourse. That is, discourse as a social practice of racism is at the same time the main source of people's racist beliefs" (p. 36). Thus the necessity to understand representations as reflecting dominant ideologies is the rationale for this research and it is by analysing the way people see Islam and Muslims *through* the media that we can begin to understand one of the factors potentially contributing to social discrimination and disadvantage amongst Muslim minorities.

---

[1] See for example, Allen and Nielsen (2002), Bunglawala, (2002) and Runnymede Trust (2001).

BACKGROUND STUDIES

REPRESENTATION OF MUSLIMS IN THE BRITISH MEDIA

Representations of Islam and Muslims in the media have been a topic of considerable debate and discussion, particularly in recent times. A substantial body of literature and research has illustrated that on the whole the images and discourses relating to Islam/Muslims in mainstream Western[2] media tend to be negative. This literature includes studies examining the concept of Orientalist discourses such as those by Said (1981 and 1996), Daniel (1960) and Sardar, (1999); the specific relationship between media and Islam, for example by Ahmed (1994), the Runnymede Trust (1997 and 2001) and Bunglawala (2002) and many recent publications including Abbas (2000), Poole (2001) and Allen (2002) which explore the prevalence of anti-Muslim and anti-Islamic opinions in the media.

BASIC THEORY AND CONCEPT OF REPRESENTATION

Such work is informed by the various theories of representation that look to understand representation as more than a romanticised mirror of life, be it by an individual artist or societal project. In such theories, media representation is strongly linked to actual reality, structures of power that inform not only cultural considerations but can and do affect concrete power structures and power relations between societal actors, particularly, as we are discussing the relationship between majority and minority /ies. Such representation and the lopsided effect of power that it creates has on many occasions arisen from misunderstanding and miscommunication.

If representation is always dominated by 'miss-representation' resulting in the misrepresentation of reality in the majority of the cases, we need to ask why. The simple answer is that we, as interpreters of 'reality', as both artist and viewer are not able to see 'reality' in its entirety or as it is intended to be seen either by cosmic or natural design or indeed that of the artist / communicator. Accordingly, one can argue that we see 'objectivities' through our 'subjectivities'. We construct reality according to previous perceptions through the channel of 'the first effect' received from 'others'. This is not a fixed impression about all, it is highly dependent on 'who is the audience' and who is the 'author'.

To try to understand representation, we need to look at it as a 'discursive structure'. The discursive approach to representation examines representation in the form of an interrelated circle of meaning. Traditionally, meaning is ascribing to objects 'out there' in the world, and to the inner essences and feelings of individuals. According to structuralists, meaning is an effect of signification, and that signification is a property not of the world out there nor of individual people, but of language, accordingly it is argued that 'we are what we say, and the world is what we say it is' (O'Sullivan, *et al.*, 1997:93).

According to Hall (1997, p. 44) the term 'discourse' is normally used as a linguistic concept, which simply means passages of connected writing, picture, speech or even socio-cultural context.

> 'By 'discourse', Foucault meant 'a group of statements which provide

---

[2] Western refers mainly to the UK, USA and Europe.

a language for talking about a way of representing the knowledge about a particular topic at a particular historical moment… Discourse is about the production of knowledge through language. But… since all social practices entail meaning and meanings shape and influence what we do, our conduct, all practices have a discursive aspect' (Hall, 1992, p. 291).

REPRESENTATION THEORIES

There are three different approaches to representation. The first theory is the '**reflective approach**' which can be considered as a reductionist understanding of representation. According to reflective representation, 'meaning is thought to lie in the object, person, idea or event in the real world, and language functions like a mirror, to reflect the true meaning as it already exists in the world. As the poet Gertrude Stein once said, "A rose is a rose is a rose". According to Hall (1997, p. 24):

> "…visual signs do bear some relationship to the shape and texture of the objects which they represent. But… a two-dimensional visual image of a rose is a sign, it should not be confused with the real plant with thorns and blooms growing in the garden. Remember also that there are many words, sounds and images which we fully well understand but which are entirely fictional or fantasy and refer to worlds which are wholly imaginary, including many people now think, most of the Iliad."

The second approach is opposite to the first, which emphasises the ordinary aspect of representation. Its focus is on an '**intentional approach**' to representation. Intentional theory gives agency to 'the speaker, the author, who imposes his or her unique meaning on the world through language. Words mean what the author intends they should mean (*ibid*, p. 25). Stuart Hall opposed intentional theory, by arguing that 'we cannot be the sole or unique source of meanings in language, since that would mean that we could express ourselves in entirely private languages. But the essence of languages is communication and that, in turn, depends on shared linguistic conventions and shared codes. Language can never be wholly a private game' (*ibid*).

The third approach is dominant discourse in representation theory called the '**constructionist approach**'. According to the constructionist approach, neither things in themselves nor the individual users of language can fix meaning in language, however this does not mean that we produce meaning. According to this approach, 'it is not the material world which conveys meaning; it is the language system or whatever system we are using to represent our concepts. It is social actors who use the conceptual systems of their culture and the linguist and other representational systems to construct meaning, to make the world meaningful and to communicate about that world meaningfully to others (*ibid*). So to understand representation constructively, one needs to find dominant discourses. It is arguable that representation cannot be precisely understood, unless it examines reality and representation in a 'discursive structure'.

It seems all three theories can be workable and inadaptable at the same time. It depends on the power and powerlessness of the reader and audience of the text. This, it seems, is the shared weakness of all three theories - the lack of attention to the power or powerlessness of the reader. If the reader is powerful in terms of removing the veil of representation i.e. informed interpretation, then the reality itself becomes more representative than the representation of reality produced by means of representation.

Understanding the core meaning of representation, discursive interpretation is inevitable, in that we can unlock the location of power within discourses that affect Muslims and the way they are represented. Here we need to characterise the dominant discourses of British Media to understand 'British Muslim Representation' in the media. Ideological representation is one of the most common discourses, particularly when it is related to religion, ethnicity and power.

Ideological representation in essence is about domination discourse – a way of making a 'privileged position' for a particular idea, value, culture and even civilization, to marginalize and mutate the rest, even to the extent of legitimizing violence against them. Ideological representation – though not always a project or effect of social engineering – nevertheless has the power to change reality according to what political system or ideological politics it wants to represent. It is arguable that ideological representation can take place in three interrelated structural discourses:

> 1. **Ethnocentric discourse:** ethnocentric discourse is about centrality of 'self', 'group' or a 'nation' reflected in e.g. the construction of, 'We are European' and a sense of being periphery for the rest. Centrism looks for segregation between 'We' and 'You' which can end in 'either you are with us or you should die' in the 18th century and 'either you are with us or against us' in the 21st century.

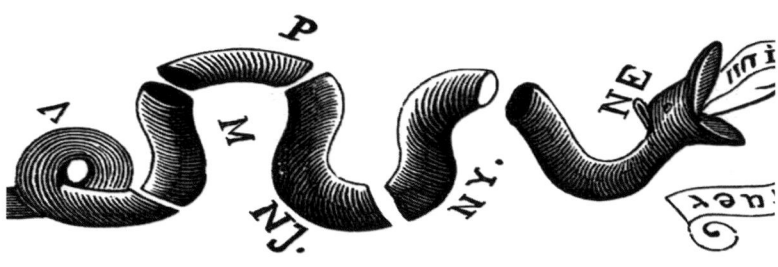

Propoganda poster from 18th century USA

> 2. **Domination discourse:** The discourse of domination is about power and influence. According to this discourse, representation of 'We" and 'Others' is about superiority of 'We' and 'weakness' and disadvantage of 'others'.

> 3. **Demonisation discourse:** Demonisation discourse is based on malicious dishonesty, hypocrisy and fantasy. Here a camera could, by reproducing some elements of reality reproduce an (un)reality according to a 'film script' or the agenda of a screenwriter and or a director. Demonisation discourse of representation explains a process of destroying a reality.

Religiophobia and ethnophobia in general and Islamophobia in particular are obvious results of 'demonisation discourse' in representing other 'religions and ethnic groups as a phobic enemy'. Sometimes Islamophobia is articulated when one is demonised by both religion and ethnicity. As a result there is double disadvantage with e.g. someone of say, Pakistani, Iranian or Iraqi origin is discriminated both the basis of their ethnicity and at the same time for being Muslim. Conversely advantage or privilege can work on a twofold level with one being both white European and non-Muslim.

MUSLIM PERCEPTIONS OF THE MEDIA

There is a dominant perception amongst Muslims that the media does indeed portray them and their religion in an inaccurate and derogatory manner;

> "The western media are largely seen by Muslims as a negative influence. This view is perhaps not without foundation. The traditional Orientalist stereotypes of Muslims as political anarchists and tyrants at home subjugating their women have been disseminated in the media as caricatures and stereotypes. Very often the news that is shown about Muslims centres around negative stories" (Ahmed, 1992, p. 9).

Certain common images and stereotypes tend to dominate both visual and print media, and hostility towards Islam combines with journalistic values and practices to create a limited caricature of the faith and its followers which continually circulates in the media. The 'preferred reading' or meaning of these discourses convey to the reader the otherness of Muslims and Islam and through these cultural myths create distance between dominant and minority groups (Hall, 1993). It is these myths and predetermined notions about minorities that contribute to a social order that dictates who participates and who does not – who 'belongs' and who is an 'outsider' (Campbell: 1995).

Nahdi (2003) talks about a "Western news agenda dominated by hostile, careless coverage of Islam [which] distorts reality and destroys trust" amongst the Muslim readership and audiences (p. 1). He notes that the general degradation in the standards of western media and journalism, with a move towards sound bites, snippets and quick and easy stories, has actually legitimised the voice of extremist Islam. This focus on extreme minority or fringe groups which represent a small section of the Muslim population, often unacceptable to other Muslims, disguises the vast diversity and range of perspectives amongst Muslims and equates the outlook and actions of a few individuals to over 1 billion people worldwide.

In his analysis of Muslims and Islam in the British press, Whitaker (2002) notes that "there are four very persistent stereotypes that crop up time and again in the different articles. These tell us that Muslims are intolerant, misogynistic, violent or cruel, and finally, strange or different" (p. 55). Again, perhaps reflecting news values as well as audience reception, he observes that Muslims are reported on mainly when they cause trouble and though "negative stories often come from other countries, they obviously have some effect on readers' perceptions of Muslims in Britain" (p. 55).

Whilst the news agendas relating to Islam and Muslims are driven by contemporary debates (geopolitical, social, cultural, economic etc), they are also fixed in historical discourses about Islam. "Today's Islamophobia feeds on history to fill out its stereotypes, but it also has features that stem from more recent narratives such as colonialism, immigration and racism" (Abbas, 2000, p. 65). In recycling the Orientalist theories about the Islamic Other, contemporary media institutions refer to Muslims and Islam in the same set of frameworks and use almost the same language to describe them, albeit with a modern spin. The survival of mediaeval concepts about Islam in western media and the canon of literature established at that time is reinforced as truth even in modern times (Daniel, 1960). Historical images of barbaric, violent, backward, intolerant Muslims, whose religious and cultural values and practices are not only different but are inherently inferior to 'ours', can still be found in the media and popular culture.

> "The language and images that the media have used in conjunction with ideas of Muslims and Islam have been value-loaded and lack context… portraying Islam as a dangerous religion rooted in violence and irrationality. While the world moves on and new ideas develop we still use the same words, in relation to Islam, that we used 10 and 20 years and even 30 years ago". (Conte, 2001)

It has been argued that certain images and stereotypes are now so deeply embedded and almost necessary to media coverage, that Islamophobia is almost a natural process (Allen, 2002). This mirrors the increase in Islamophobic incidents and general attitudes now present in British society (Ameli *et al*, 2004a, 2004b, 2006a, 2006b). In exploring the 'language of Islamophobia', Henzell-Thomas (2001) names particular discursive structures and strategies that can be commonly found in texts. These include repetition, hyperbole, ridicule, metaphor, blaming the victim, and use of assumptions and 'taken for granted' presuppositions about the subject. This can be compared to the 'acceptable' or 'common sense' racism that can also be found in the media (Hall, 1993).

The 'otherness' of Muslims is clearly evident in contemporary discourse but they are not biologically inferior as they were in the times of 'old' racism, they are simply different, having a different culture. This 'new' racism is of a subtle and symbolic nature; it is discursive and is expressed in text and everyday talk (van Dijk, 2000). Representations of Muslims as the 'enemy within', disloyal or 'fifth columnists' are rife – some subtle and some not even attempting to disguise their aversion to the presence of Muslim communities in the West.

> "The media in Britain continues to reinforce Islamophobic attitudes in the majority community. In addition many Islamic movements, as well as Western Islamophobia, have helped create a perception that Muslims share few civic values with other faiths and traditions in Britain: that they are not sincere in their acceptance of democracy, pluralism and human rights. Government and other mainstream politicians also use a vocabulary that has the potential to generate fear, threats and antipathy towards British Muslims". (Ansari, 2002, p24)

Richardson's (2001) empirical study of representations of British Muslims in the broadsheet press suggests that; "(i) British Muslim communities are almost wholly absent from the news, excluded from all but predominantly negative contexts; (ii) when British Muslims do appear, they are included only as participants in news events, not as providers of informed commentary on news events; and therefore (iii) that the issues and concerns of the communities are not being served by the agendas of the broadsheet press". This absence from the media relates to concepts developed in 'muted group theory' whereby certain groups in society are muted – either silent, not heard or only able to speak a language imposed by others (Kramarae, 1981). This language has been constructed to describe minority groups, including Muslims, and speaks to the powerful majority who control aspects of cultural representation, but it may have little or no meaning to Muslims themselves. Unless challenged, debate and discussion can only take place using this dominant ideological language, which inevitably results in a muted or limited response from less powerful groups in a dialogue that was not based on an equal footing.

An example of this can be found in the use of words such as *'jihad'* which have been appropriated by the media to mean something very specific and different from the concept as understood by many Muslims. Discussion around the issue of *hijab* is another example illustrating the restrictive nature of language and discourse which leads readers to predetermined outcomes rather than enabling them to engage in genuine debate. Highlighting a Muslim woman's dress code as being 'different' from that of a secular Western woman, debate is automatically confined to specific terms leaving no room for alternative readings. This difference is shown to be inferior, of less value and in fact unnecessary and therefore problematic. The underlying questions being asked include 'why must Muslim women insist on wearing *hijab* when other women don't?' 'Why is it that Muslims have so much trouble accepting and adopted our values and dressing accordingly?' Whilst this does not ignore an audience's ability to interpret meanings in oppositional or negotiated ways, it signals that media 'texts' are read in broader contexts of cultural understandings and consensus. Only when language shifts away from dominant narratives appealing to the majority – innately marginalising minorities – can there be communication on an open and equal basis.

It is widely acknowledged that there was a great increase in reports about Islam and Muslims following events in September 2001. For instance, figures compiled by Whitaker (2002) are reproduced in Table 1, showing the phenomenal increase in the number of articles containing the word 'Muslim'[3] before and after September 2001[4].

Table 1: Articles containing the word 'Muslim'

Newspaper	2000-2001	2001-2002	% Increase
Guardian	817	2,043	250
Independent	681	1,556	228
Times	535	1,486	278
Telegraph	417	1,176	282
Mail	202	650	322
Mirror	164	920	561
Express	139	305	219
Sun	80	526	658
Star	40	144	360

Unsurprisingly, the broadsheets, especially *The Guardian* and *The Independent* showed more interest in Islam/Muslims both before and after the event but the increase in every newspaper was dramatic.

---

[3] The spelling 'Moslem' was also used in his search.

[4] The 12 month period between early September 2000 and 2001 compared with 19 June 2001 to 19 June 2002.

Work carried out for the Muslim Council of Britain (MCB) analysed reporting in 6 newspapers[5] before and after 11th September 2001 and gauged the frequency of use of certain words and phrases. All newspapers used phrases containing the word Islamic or Muslim in the reports on the following day, 12th September 2001. Each newspaper tended to have a particular way of describing who it thought were the culprits, for example, Islamic extremist, Islamic fanatics or Islamic fundamentalists or fundamentalism, and tended to use this phrase more than others, although other similar terms were used within the same article.

The use of any of these phrases may not have been frequent within any one article but it normally had the desired effect of turning the reader's attention toward a particular idea or phenomenon. In *The Sun* for example, although the occurrence of phrases was relatively low, they would occur in the opening paragraphs such that a framework was established within which to read the rest of the article. If it had originally stated that 'Islamic fundamentalists' were responsible for the attacks, later words like fundamentalist, extremist, Afghani fundamentalist or fundamentalist Afghani regime may have been used interchangeably to denote the same people. The 'lexical choice' of words and phrases within a particular context enables readers to gain from it implicit understandings and meanings, especially in relation to minorities and more often than not these meanings are negative (van Dijk, 2000).

It is however important to differentiate between articles which were more restrained in not only their use of the chosen phrases but which gave a balanced argument of the incident. For example, two articles may both have contained the same phrase but the context may have been very different. One may have looked at the reasons why America was a target of this type of terrorist activity whereas the other may have talked about the nature of the Taliban and Osama bin Laden. However, it would not be an overstatement to say that in many people's minds the use of words such as 'Islamic extremist' would simply have reinforced negative stereotypes regardless of the context of articles. The greatest impact of this kind of press reporting has probably been to inflate the potential danger which 'Islamic extremists' pose to the Western world. Frequent use of the above phrases no doubt reinforced previously held prejudices and fears about the Islamic world and Muslims living in the West.

These attitudes and representations are evident in many western countries with Muslim populations. Elmasry (2002) demonstrates how in the Canadian media, especially after 9/11, "the frequent demonic portrayal and misrepresentation of Islam and Muslims has been one of the most persistent, virulent and socially significant sources of anti-Islam" (p 58). His identification of the coupling of words such as 'extremist', 'fundamentalist' and 'terrorist' with Islam or Muslim, shows a disturbing development in reporting in both print and broadcast media. Research in Europe has also reached similar conclusions recognising the media in 15 EU states as being one of the most obvious sources of Islamophobic attitudes and ideas (Allen & Neilsen, 2002). Whilst this study concludes that it is difficult to assess comprehensively whether the media impacted positively or negatively in light of reporting after September 2001, it asserts "the media's role cannot be overlooked, and it has

---

[5] The Daily Telegraph, The Times (Sunday Times), The Mirror, The Express, The Daily Mail (Mail on Sunday) and The Sun (News of the World) were selected for analysis. A content analysis was carried out from 4-25th September 2001 enabling a comparison of a week before and two weeks after September 11th

been identified as having an inherent negativity towards Muslims and Islam" (p 47). Examples of balanced and objective reporting in European media were also cited in this work.

From the UK perspective, British Muslims' views were reported, specifically whether there was support for 9/11 attacks and for subsequent US military action against Afghanistan. The possibility of recruits from amongst British Muslims for an impending 'holy war' was also examined. 'Networks' of potential terrorists in the UK were investigated and this linked into how similar acts could be prevented in the future, not just in the US but in Britain too. Immigration policies were put under scrutiny and the issue of identity cards was raised. *The Sun*, with its almost obsessive coverage of immigration, tied the two issues together, heightening concerns of bogus asylum seekers and now potentially deadly foreigners.

Another research project[6] examined the television news coverage of the events in September 2001 and aimed to ascertain audiences' reactions to this. Whilst confirming other research findings about descriptions of Muslims as barbaric, medieval and poor; against the Christian West as civilised, democratic and affluent; the study found that:

> "A deep lack of trust in British and American TV news was evident in the views expressed among most British Muslim informants. The commonest complaints concerned lack of challenging debate, sensationalist reporting, limited and limiting frameworks and perspectives, and anti-Arab and anti-Muslim assumptions".

Many of the respondents felt that the news media failed to represent the full range and plurality of views of UK citizens, especially Muslims and those speaking Arabic. This resonates with other studies which show that marginal, though vociferous, so-called extremist views are over-represented at the expense of the more subtle and nuanced perspectives of many Muslims.

Clearly any analysis of media representations of Islam and Muslims needs to acknowledge that examples of positive or balanced stories do exist and that whilst overall the media is seen as unsympathetic towards Islam, there has been space within different outlets to articulate challenging or alternative discourses, often by Muslims themselves[7]. These more discerning articles and programmes not only provided information about Muslim communities and their faith at the time when there was immense interest about them but they also established channels for ongoing discussion pertaining to relevant issues. For instance, *The Guardian* website has a link to pages of articles and information including special reports about Muslims in its 'British Muslims' section. The BBC news website, whilst dedicating pages to all religions, has a diverse set of contemporary topics including discussion forums relating to Islam and Muslims. Similarly Channel 4 has kept information about its 'Islam Season' active on its website. Bunglawala (2002) cites similar media coverage:

---

[6]

After September 11: TV News and Transnational Audiences. Jointly funded by the Broadcasting Standards Commission (BSC), the Independent Television Commission (ITC), the British Film Institute (BFI), Open University – National Everyday Cultures Programme (OU/NECP) and the Economic Social Research Council (ESRC) Transnational Communities Research Programme.

[7]

For example the editors of *The Muslim News* and *Q-News* have written articles in *The Independent* and *The Guardian*.

"In a supportive two-page editorial spread, [*The Sun*] declared that, 'Islam is not an evil religion' and urged Britons to be more sensitive to Muslims concerns about stereotyping. *The Daily Telegraph* published a special 16-page colour supplement to inform its readers about basic Islamic beliefs and teachings, while *The Guardian* ran a week long Muslim Britain series which was perhaps the most extensive and positive look at the British Muslim community that had yet appeared in a national newspaper in the UK" (p. 50).

Recognising this diversity within the media is important as it enables a fairer analysis of the types and variety of representations being made[8]. It does not however, detract from the fact that even some of the discourses utilised in the 'liberal' media can include Islamophobic attitudes. Allen (2005) compares BNP rhetoric with the musings of writers in broadsheets such as *The Guardian* and *The Independent*. Ignorance and misrepresentation of sacred texts; denial of the existence of Islamophobia – and in fact seeing Muslims themselves as a threat to Britain, and opinions of politicians from left and right, all demonstrated the predominance of anti-Islamic and anti-Muslim prejudice across a range of political thought and in a variety of different public arenas.

 Will Britain Convert to Islam?

Peter Hitchens, Mail on Sunday, November 02 2003

The idea of an Islamic Britain may seem highly unlikely now, amid what still seems to be more or less a Western, Christian society. We are used to thinking of Islam as a religion of backward regions, and of backward people. But we should remember that Muslim armies came within inches of taking Vienna in 1683 and were only driven from Spain in 1492. In those days it was the Islamic world that was making the great scientific advances which we now assume are ours by right

The Country that hates itself

Melanie Phillips, Canadian Post, June 16 2006

Like Canada, Britain prides itself on being a tolerant society committed to minority rights. Yet in the wake of the July bombings, the U.K. government estimated that 26% of Britain's 1.6 million Muslims felt no loyalty to Britain, 3,000 had passed through al Qaeda camps and up to 16,000 were either actively engaged in or supported terrorist activity.

In Britain, this warped thinking led many to say after 9/11 that the United States 'had it coming.' After last year's suicide bombings in London in which more than 50 British citizens were murdered by British Islamists, Muslims complained that talk about Islamic terrorism was Islamophobia and therefore taboo - and Britain's political and security establishment supinely agreed.

---

[8] Hall (1997) talks about this in relation to the representation of race and race issues.

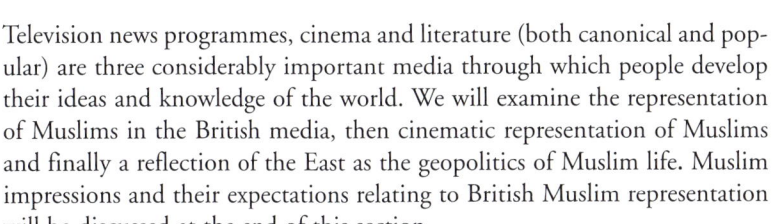

Limp Liberals fail to protect their most profound values

Polly Toynbee, The Guardian, October 10 2001

Despite sects and schisms, Islam is united in feeling threatened and it is not just extremists on the streets of Pakistan and Palestine, it is almost everyone. For Britain this has a lethal potential. It underlines how alienated most still feel from the mainstream, how threatened, how culturally uncertain. Unfortunately it unites the peaceful with the violent.

Television news programmes, cinema and literature (both canonical and popular) are three considerably important media through which people develop their ideas and knowledge of the world. We will examine the representation of Muslims in the British media, then cinematic representation of Muslims and finally a reflection of the East as the geopolitics of Muslim life. Muslim impressions and their expectations relating to British Muslim representation will be discussed at the end of this section,.

DOMINATION, DEMONISATION OR BOTH?
THE 'COMMON SENSE' OF TELEVISION NEWS
AND CINEMA

Television news consists of a number of factors which differentiate it from other forms of news and media and it is for these reasons that it has been chosen for analysis. The first and most important of these is its high audience figures and the general reliance placed on television news to inform quickly, accurately and continuously which make it one of the most important sources of information available to our society today (Lewis, 1995). Broadcast news is able to provide up-to-date news and information – news as it breaks, 24 hours a day – which differentiates it from daily press news. "For most people in Britain, television news remains the most pervasive and most trusted source of information about the world. Television news is generally given greater credence by the public than either newspapers or radio; probably because it is perceived to be less partisan than the press and because it offers the 'evidence' of pictures that isn't available on radio" (Goodwin & Whannel, 1995, p. 42). The particular characteristic of presenting news in visual as well as oral form is obviously one of the most important aspects of television news. The visual signs include all the images and graphics that are seen on screen and combine these with oral signs of speech, sound and music.

Television is an iconic medium rather than simply a symbolic one. "The conventions of representation on television most often rely on the iconic nature of images to convey an impression of realism. This realism is understood because the audience accept the conventions of composition, perspective and framing which are so embedded in Western culture that the two-dimensional image seems simply to convey three-dimensional reality" (Bignell, 2004, p. 87). However, this denotation of the real world is far from a neutral or objective exercise and the production of television, including news, involves certain professional norms, industry practices and conventions of meaning-making that have been adopted by both the makers and audiences of television. In this way the producers of news programmes rely on unconscious knowledge of codes which the audiences possess as well as their ability to decode signs – by understanding their connotations – and assemble them into meaningful messages.

As the work of the Glasgow University Media Group (GUMG) amongst others, has shown, news is never neutral or objective but always shows bias. Through various studies they have demonstrated that the hierarchical structure within which media institutions operate and the close links they have with a range of official and accepted sources result in the news giving preferential treatment to certain ways of seeing the world and draw on a narrow range of views that tend to favour the rich and powerful[9]. According to Fiske (2003) there is a need to "demystify news's discursive strategies and discredit its ideology of objectivity and truth" (p. 308). The notion of balance and objectivity claimed by television news can only be defined in relation to common-sense assumptions held consensually in society but these common-sense views have at some point become naturalised ideological positions and norms that are themselves cultural constructs and not 'truth'.

Whilst the news is arguably a 'window on the world', this window places reality within a frame that has been imposed on the scene and has selected which aspect of reality to convey. Television news always transmits a symbolic representation of, a message about, reality, which is not so much a reflection of reality as an interpretation of it (Hall, 1975). Additionally Hall asserts that each single act of selection is saturated by social values and attitudes through which a dominant minority speaks to the majority. Indeed there have been strong criticisms of television news on both sides of the Atlantic. Some of this criticism has focused on coverage of events of major international or political significance, for example the military action in Iraq, whilst other commentators have scrutinised domestic news (Raboy & Dagenais, 1992). Kellner (1992) argues that an increasing corporate control of media constitutes a 'crisis of democracy' and further concentrates the control of news production in the hands of fewer, more powerful people and organisations. "Not only are news programmes slanted towards the hegemonic position of corporate and government elite, but discussion shows that they are also dominated by conservative discourse" (Kellner, 1992, p. 51). Corporate control restricts and stifles debate and when oppositional voices are presented, in an effort to maintain balance, it is done so within a framework set by powerful producers. The overall limits of debate are predetermined and any contradictory or alternative views appear as fragmented and are not explored as rational alternative explanations (Philo, *et al*, 1982). This omission resonates with the ideas in muted group theory, such that production processes, structures, language and frames are set up to disadvantage or marginalise – if not totally suppress – minority voices and agendas.

Television news then has specific characteristics which differentiates it from other news media, but along with all news media as a genre, sets it apart from genres such as cinema. News is perceived as a medium reflecting reality and is therefore read on these terms whereas cinema and film does not carry the myth of objectivity or of representing the truth : film is openly and recognisably fiction. "Television, by contrast, consistently reproduces the events, actors, manners and interactions of everyday life – its subject matter is, so frequently, the subject of 'reality', that we are constantly tempted to believe that it has no intrinsic mode of signification at all – that it is a discourse without conventions" (Hall, 1975 p. 102).

---

[9] Philo, et al (1982).

One profound difference between fictional media such as cinema and the 'factual' realm of television news is that (Bignell, 2004, p. 93):

> "…news narrative contributes to the process of constructing a common-sense climate of opinion through which audiences perceive their reality. Therefore television news shares with other news media (such as newspapers and radio) the ideological function of naturalising the assumptions that day-to-day occurrences in the public arenas of politics, business and international affairs are what are most important about the daily affairs of a society"

That is not to say films and fiction do not have an impact on people's knowledge acquisition or in determining what we regard as culturally acceptable and or normal. Over the past few years in particular, there has been considerable concern, indeed alarm, at the way Hollywood films have portrayed and cast Arabs and Muslims (Shaheen, 2003). As a primary instrument in communicating social and cultural values and attitudes, Hollywood can be seen as a globally influential force, different from news yet still having a far reaching impact.

Mistry (1999) argues that the idea of hegemony is of particular salience to the exploration of racial representations in the media because television and cinema are both central to popular culture and are seen as 'everyday' routine or 'common sense' values. Thus, whilst being different in certain ways, these two media need to be considered in trying to locate the 'mechanisms of domination'. Though Mistry focused on the representation of 'racial' groups, the principles she outlines are relevant to other minority groups, including Muslims.

As noted above, the ultimate question of concern to this study is the impact or potential influence of representations on individual readers/viewers and thus wider society. Whilst media texts can be analysed for what they probably denote, it is not until we study the parallel part of the process – the connotation – that we can appreciate the complete chain of communication. In Hall's (1994) four-stage theory of communication; production, circulation, use (which he calls distribution or consumption) and reproduction; we are most interested in reproduction. Production and reproduction of messages are not identical but they are related and only when messages are appropriated as meaningful discourses by an audience can they be meaningfully decoded. Hall (1994, p. 43) states:

> "It is this set of decoded meanings which 'have an effect', influence, entertain, instruct or persuade, with very complex perceptual, cognitive, emotional and ideological or behavioural consequences. In a 'determinate' moment the structure employs a code and yields a 'message': at another determinate moment the 'message', via its decoding, issues into the structure of social practices".

Before any meaning can be taken from messages there has to exist a set of naturalised codes or natural recognitions for which the encoder-producer assumes will translate into naturalised perceptions for the decoder-receiver, only then has a meaningful exchange taken place.

So for example, when news refers to 'Islamic fundamentalist', the phrase is denoted with a particular set of meanings and values, the connotations of which are decoded by the majority of the audience in a certain way. These will reflect the existing knowledge and dominant meanings associated with the term in relation to religion, people, actions and ideologies. From these a dominant or preferred reading will be made and according to Hall, (1994, p. 51):

> "...[the] domain of preferred meanings has a whole social order embedded in them as a set of meanings, practices and beliefs: the everyday knowledge of social structures, of 'how things work for all practical purposes in this culture', the rank order of power and interest and the structure of legitimacy, limits and sanctions".

Though there may be different readings of discourse or messages, namely dominant-hegemonic, negotiated and oppositional (Hall, 1994), the first of these is of particular relevance to the reception of media texts about Islam and Muslims. The definition of dominant-hegemonic viewpoint (Hall, 1994, p. 50) is:

> "(a) that it defines within its terms the mental horizon, the universe, of possible meanings, of a whole sector of relations in a society or culture; and (b) that it carries with it the stamp of legitimacy – it appears coterminous with what is 'natural', 'inevitable', 'taken for granted' about social order".

It is possible for viewers to adopt negotiated or even oppositional readings using the idea of selective perception (which according to Hall is never as selective, random or privatised as the term suggests) but 'cognitive balance theory' suggests people avoid absorbing information which contradicts or conflicts with knowledge already held (Graber, 1988). Conversely, it follows that by absorbing information which resonates with their previous learning; people reinforce their opinions and in a cyclical process of (re)confirmation find their views endorsed by media discourse.

In applying these ideas to the examination of media descriptions of Islam and Muslims, if no meaning is taken, there can be no consumption and if the meaning is not articulated in practice, it has no effect (Hall, 1975). However, if it is consumed and articulated, Islamophobic discourse could impact on the way non-Muslims perceive and interact with Muslims. If terms such as '*jihad*', 'fundamentalist', '*hijab*' etc are encoded with negative and threatening meanings then there are real possibilities for definable social effects resulting from the circulation of these ideas. These social effects can operate at the individual level as well as at the institutional level where they will no doubt have greater repercussions for Muslim communities as a whole.

OTHERNESS, THE ORIENT, ISLAM AND MUSLIMS: UNDERSTANDING THE ROLE AND EFFECT OF LITERATURE AND CINEMA ON SOCIETY AND SOCIAL ACTORS

This understanding of the interplay of representations of Muslims with the (negative) social experiences of Muslims can be understood further by contextualising the construction of Oriental otherness. As discussed initially in this work, representation, be it the storyline of a soap opera, a painting, film documentary or drama or TV or print news, is usually understood to be faithful to the original. However, representation is largely interwoven with many other things besides 'truth'. It is defined not just by inherent common subject matter, but also by a common history, tradition, and universe of discourse that exist within a particular field. Whilst having non-European geographical meaning, the Orient is the land east of Europe which is usually understood through the writings of Western artists, travellers, or 'experts' on the region. Orientalism, on the other hand, describes the various schools of thought and methods of investigation through which this knowledge of the East came into being. According to scholars such as Professor Edward Said, it is through ideas of the Orient and the operation of Orientalism via Western discourses, that the West has been able to legitimize and maintain its hold over the uncivilized 'Other'. That 'other' includes the internal 'other' the Orient as represented by the Behranis, Saids etc. of Western nations (see analysis below)

As exemplified in the film analysis below and as will be discussed with reference to canonical and popular literary fiction, a major and repeated feature of Oriental analysis in all its various forms is that it constantly confirms the thesis that the Oriental is primitive, mysterious, exotic and incapable of rational self-government.

However, Orientalism should not be looked upon as merely the rationalization of colonial rule and racism. Far more important, it seems, is how it knowingly or unknowingly justifies colonialism, imperialism, and neo-imperialism in advance of their actual manifestations.

In other words, "Orientalism is best viewed in Foucauldian terms as a discourse: a manifestation of power/knowledge" (Ashcroft & Ahluwalia, 1999, p. 68) or a severely bounded area of social knowledge. This is because, as Foucault sees it, discourse is a severely bounded area of social knowledge or "heavily policed cognitive systems which control and delimit both the mode and the means of representation in a given society" (Gandhi, 1998, p. 77). Its recognition is brought into being through discourse, which is ideologically loaded, but independent of individual will and judgment. Demonisation again, though part of a cultural and clearly imperialistic and colonial project, again becomes detached from the original intention as it pervades and informs other forms of representation in a supposedly post-colonial era and culture. So whereas, manifest Orientalism is basically comprised of openly stated ideas about Eastern civilization, history, government, or literature produced at different historical junctures, latent Orientalism is an "almost unconscious and certainly an untouchable positivity" (Childs & Williams, 1997, p. 101) that:

> "[…] contains the basic 'truths' of the Orient, so that while, for example historians might disagree about particular interpretations of the history of the Orient, underlying assumptions of oriental backwardness would remain unquestioned. As such latent Orientalism has strong affinities with certain concepts of ideology, particularly the 'negative' version of ideology as false consciousness, and the durability of ideological formations, especially when allied to strong institutions such as Orientalism, would also help to explain the survival of Orientalist attitudes (Childs & Williams, 1997, p. 101-02)."

According to Said (1981) Orientalist discourse is the system of thought by which dominant economic, social, cultural, and political powers establish spheres of 'knowledge' and 'truth' and it is through such discursive practices that religions, races, cultures, and classes are represented. These discursive practices are interwoven with social and power relations, while history itself is indivisible from social formations.

Western representations of the 'Orient' or Muslims in general is a phenomenon created by writers, intellectuals, artists, commentators, travellers, as well as others working within similar discursive formations.

What brings 'Western' texts from separate intellectual disciplines as well as different historical eras together as a single discourse called Orientalism, is the common culture and ideology intrinsic to the discursive practices through which they produce knowledge about the Orient. These powerful discursive practices make it difficult for individuals to think beyond them. A *demonised oriental / Muslim* 'other' is understood as the normal(ised) oriental/

Muslim 'other' and the question of critically examining such representation is a non-starter in the minds of an audience which understands such representation to be the given upon which to base their better understanding of a text / film etc.

However, it should be kept in mind that this does not mean that (an) Orientalist discourse is either completely static or cannot admit internal contradictions. It is often the case that Orientalist modes of thought and representation are actually able to survive contact with the reality on the ground with which it often seems to be at odds. One reason for this may be that the need for creating an overall consistency in discourse may constantly prevent the realization of objective analysis as well as commitment to 'truth'. The stronger the discourse becomes, the longer it lives and the better it is able to bring about consistency within its borders. This is helped through the continued repetition and adaptation of its motifs. Another explanation for the persistent Orientalist mode of representation is Said's concept of latent and manifest Orientalism, as discussed above, where latent Orientalism informs the givens upon which often self-consciously post-colonial audiences still ground their knowledge base from.

It is important to note that even Orientalist literature that makes no claim to authenticity. It mediates between the real and imaginary worlds and can often be seen as a form of latent Orientalism. As ideologies intersect and battle one another through language and signs, all literary texts must be viewed "as extremely fecund sites for such ideological interactions" (Loomba, 1998, p. 70). Indeed, it seems inevitable that "texts or representations have to be seen as fundamental to the creation of history and culture" (Loomba, 1998, p. 40).

An important aspect of Said's *Orientalism* is that it explains the methods through which a monolithic 'Other' was constructed by the West as its barbaric, despotic, and inferior opposite or alter ego. It is a type of surrogate and underground version of the West or the 'self' (Macfie, 2002). What may be even more significant is that through its position of domination, the West is even able to tell the 'truth' to non-Western cultures about their past and present condition, as they are capable of representing the Orient more 'authentically' than the Orient itself. Such a 'truthful' representation not only aids the colonizer or imperialist in justifying their actions, but it also serves to weaken the resistance of 'the Other' as it changes the way in which 'the Other' views itself. Although this discourse is generated in the Occident, its influence is so powerful that it has significant impact on discursive practices in the Orient as well. The 'Other' may come to see himself and his surroundings as inferior or even barbaric. At the very least it can create a major crisis in the consciousness of 'the Other' as it clashes with powerful discursive practices and 'knowledges' about the world. Eurocentrism and ethnocentric discourse, as a result, influences, alters and even helps produce 'Other' cultures.

The impact of Orientalised discourse upon the 'Other' informs Muslim / Islamic driven critique in the UK of government and media discourses on Muslims and integration. Both Hewitt and Abdul Wahid (Q-News, July 2006) decry attempts to foist acceptable Muslim identities onto Muslims in the UK through media and government discourse and often specific initiatives. Hewitt's description of the post 7-7 Muslim experience in the UK calls for Muslims in the UK: "to stop apologising and stand up proudly for who we are and what we believe in." Criticising the ethnocentric discourse of occidental superiority post 9-11 and the attempts to impose versions of Islam onto Muslims, Hewitt states:

> "We don't have to march to Washington's tune, like Judas goats…because despite everything, 'we still have many freedoms in

Britain'. We don't have to accept false choices. After 9/11 and July 7, 2005 we were told to pick sides – "You are either with us, or with the terrorists" – dissent was unacceptable… Sorry, Mr. Bush, but I can be against you and the terrorists and still be a responsible member of society. Ditto, Mr. Blair."

The themes of loyalty to transnational causes – of the *ummah* above nation state form the basis of prejudicial representation of Muslims in films e.g. The Siege and Executive Decision and as Hewitt points out these also inform current political discourses on Muslims. This two choice option – with us or against us or as Abdul Wahid describes it: 'dictatorship' or 'secular democracy' in the Muslim world, is an 'absurdity' that is once more foisted onto Muslims who in the Muslim world, 'deserve the right to implement their own political path free from the external interference that merely sustains or tinkers with existing corrupt regimes.'

The Oriental other then can be identified not only in cinematic terms but is intrinsically part of cultural understandings of Muslim that permeate foreign policy, TV news, and domestic social policy.

METHODOLOGY

This report follows a sociological approach based on a quantitative survey and qualitative interviews. The quantitative questionnaire was part of a major survey carried out by the IHRC and reported in the first volume of 'British Muslims' Expectations of the Government : *Dual Citizenship: British, Islamic or both?* (Ameli & Merali, 2004), the second volume *Social Discrimination: Across the Muslim Divide* (Ameli *et al*, 2004),the third volume, *Secular or Islamic: What Schools do British Muslims want for their Children?* (Ameli *et al*. 2005), the fourth volume *Hijab, Meaning, Identity, Otherization and Politics: British Muslim Women* (Ameli *et al*, 2006) and the fifth volume *Law and British Muslims: Domination of the Majority or Process of Balance* (Ameli *et al* 2006).

A detailed description about participants and their demography has been offered in Volume One. Here follows a summary. The total number of quantitative responses came to 1125, with some 800 being collated by hand, and the rest through a widely publicised on-line facility, over a three-week period. The majority of them are male (64%), with slightly over one-third female (36%). They are from diverse ethnic backgrounds and the level of their religiosity and identification with Islam is also diverse, ranging from devout practitioners to cultural and secular Muslims. About 90 percent of the participants are British citizens and more than half of them (55%) are born in Britain.

About 43 percent of the respondents are employed, while the rest of the participants fall into the categories of the unemployed, self-employed and students. The sample group includes respondents from England, Scotland and Wales; approximately half (47%) of them live in London.

We also interviewed 52 Muslims from England, Scotland and Wales of whom 24 identified themselves as female and 23 as male. Respondents came from various places including various parts of inner London, Batley, Birmingham, Bradford, Edinburgh, Lincoln, Liverpool, Manchester, Nottingham and Halifax. The ethnic origins of interviewees were also diverse and included Bangladeshi, Indian, Pakistani, West Indian, Iraqi, East African Asian, Kashmiri, mixed Arab / white, and Afghan.

Respondents were asked their views on media reporting on Muslims, Muslim portrayal in the film industry, non-Muslim perception of Muslims as a result of media representation and how much opportunity is given to Muslims to express their opinions in the media.

Further to the data collected, analyses and case studies of news media, Hollywood films and classic and modern literature have also been carried out to provide additional insight into varying forms of media.

A two-week content analysis of four mainstream news programmes of BBC News, Newsnight, ITV News and Channel 4 News were undertaken prior to the events of the 7th July. The language of news media was particularly focused on throughout the analyses. The frequency of selected words was tabulated and presents comparisons between the various news programmes.

Six Hollywood films (*The Siege, Executive Decision, Raiders of the Lost Ark, House of Sand and Fog, East is East and Aladdin*) covering a range of genres (thriller, adventure, comedy, animation, and drama) were analysed linguistically and contextually.

Furthermore, an array of literature ranging from various classical works to more recent publications were also analysed focusing on Orientalist and Eurocentric discourses.

RESEARCH AND FINDINGS

As we have already discussed, the intertwining of historical narrative, majority political language and representation of the Muslim / Oriental other form part of a discourse that creates strong power relations where the majority is not only physically superior through numerical supremacy in a Western context, it is intellectually and morally superior than the demonised 'other'. What the public (non-Muslim and often Muslim) understand about Muslims in general and British Muslims in particular is thus deeply related to 'British Muslim representation' not only in the media but also in the entire social systems of the West. Representation is not simply perception; reader and audience have a critical role in creating a discursive understanding which creates, replicates and perpetuates inequalities. This is why non- British Muslims and British Muslims sometimes have dissimilar understandings of Muslim representation in the media.

PART ONE: TEXTUAL ANALYSIS - REPRESENTATION OF MUSLIM IN MEDIA TEXT

With Orientalist ideas still dominating Western media, the first part of the analysis focuses on television news, English literature and Hollywood films with the aim to expose such misrepresentations of Islam and Muslims which exist within these forms of media.

REPRESENTATION OF MUSLIMS IN BRITISH TELEVISION NEWS

In order to understand the extent to which this prejudiced and inaccurate portrayal continues in mainstream media, this research presents an analysis of television news following the London bombings in July 2005 and of selected cinema films. A two-week[10] content analysis of four television news programmes (BBC, ITV, C4 and BBC2's Newsnight) was undertaken in this study. As well as presenting an overall understanding of the discourses being articulated in the news about Islam and Muslims, a framework of selected words and phrases provided a comparison between the different news programmes[11].

There were a number of similarities in the news coverage and the terminology used by all four news sources. Some of the most frequently occurring words in all programmes were 'terrorism/t', 'suicide bomber/bomb(er)', 'police' (relating to the investigations) and the names of the suspects of the attempted bombings on 21st July and the actual 7th July bombing (See Table 2). Newsnight and Channel 4 news presented a greater depth and range of news items and dedicated time to more informed analysis in comparison with the BBC and ITV news. The news coverage will be analysed below using a number of themes (for more details see Appendix 1).

Table 2:	Frequently Occurring Words			
	BBC	Newsnight	ITV	C4
Terrorism	6	25	11	21
Suicide Bomber	14	23	28	15
Police	16	12	9	17
Names	13	8	15	21

Of the topical clusters produced by Poole (2002) most of the news coverage fell into the one on 'threat to national security/political threat'. This was perhaps not surprising considering the nature of the event, though all of the subjects listed in Poole's cluster were not of significance, for example, 'peaceful protest', 'Muslim Parliament' or 'Rise of Islam'. Furthermore there was an additional set of topics present relating more directly to the bombings, particularly, 'terrorist/extremist', 'foreign policy', 'global links' and 'bomb'.

The more varied and detailed news reports (mainly C4 and Newsnight) also developed a socio-cultural grouping which focused on issues such as:

- Muslim/non-Muslim relations
- Muslim community
- British Muslims
- Alienation/segregation
- Assimilation
- Role of mosques
- Islamophobia

---

[10] Between 25 July and 5 August 2005, though data is missing for some days.

[11] See Appendix A for analysis chart.

Though words and phrases such as 'Muslim or Islamic fundamentalist, terrorist or extremist were used surprisingly infrequently, the association with the religion of Islam and its adherents was still considerably strong. This was for at least two reasons. The first is that there is already a perceived link between Islam or Muslims and terrorism in the minds of many people because of ongoing media coverage, a recent and very significant factor being the attacks in September 2001 in the USA (Ansari, 2002). Therefore it did not require an explicit connection to be made by media sources for people to generate underlying assumptions and stereotypes. The relationship between the media and the portrayal of Islam and Muslims provides a context within which to investigate the use of seemingly neutral words and objective statements (Said, 1980). The second, more specific to the reporting of the July bombings, is that coverage immediately after the event made enough references to Islam/Islamic/Muslim and also to Al-Qaeda, that public opinion was influenced by this and any further coverage or discussion was framed within these parameters and implicitly made reference to these assumptions.

The limited frameworks (Poole, 2002) within which Islam is almost always framed in the media, means that people already have a particular set of opinions and ideas about it – very often these are negative. Thus when news of this nature breaks, these 'dormant' perceptions are triggered and even if the words 'Islam' or 'Muslim' are not used, there is an understanding or assumption of the link. In the case of reporting of July 7, 2005, when Muslim names were used at an early stage of news coverage, the connections were made in the minds of most viewers and readers. It could be argued that the media had no choice but to make public the names of the suspects and that it was not in their control of whether these would be Muslim names or not, but what is being explored here is the overall impact of the coverage.

The nature of the event necessitated that certain details were provided and as such particular words were used frequently. These words, for instance, 'bomb', 'police', 'security', legislation' and the names of people and places, can be seen as a logical or practical aspect of news reporting, in which some basic facts have to be conveyed. Though even the language used in this case reflects on news values and the nature of news production, it is arguably less subjective and value-laden than terms such as 'radical', 'terrorist' or 'extremist'. However, though it has been noted that phrases such as 'Islamic fundamentalist' were used *infrequently*, they were nonetheless used. This use, limited though it was, makes a direct and obvious link between the religion of Islam and its followers and motivations as well as justifications for acts of terror.

ASYLUM AND IMMIGRATION

One of the dominant themes in all of the coverage was asylum and immigration. Some reports placed considerable emphasis on the backgrounds of the suspected bombers, describing how they had sought asylum in the UK some years prior to the event, had either been or were in the process of being granted indefinite leave to stay or citizenship and had now partaken in these acts of violence on British soil. The nature of their new lives, mainly that they had received an education, financial support, housing and similar benefits, were all outlined. This type of representation was similar to tabloid depictions of 'benefit scroungers' living off the state and often averse to that very state[12]. Closely linked to the debate around asylum and immigration was that of

---

12

In the case of Muslims, most notoriously used to describe Omar Bakri Mohammed, leader of Al-Muhajiroun, but also other political refugees such as Abu Hamza.

deportation. Deporting foreign nationals, including asylum seekers who were awaiting a decision on their application but were found to be involved in such illegal activities, was presented as one option for the authorities to combat the threat of terrorism – and presumably to appease those who thought Britain was being 'swamped' by foreigners. Whilst reintroducing the controversial question of asylum/immigration back onto the agenda, this argument also reinforced the foreign or alien nature of Islam/Muslims. However, as one commentator noted it was easy to fall into 'comfort zones' and blame everything on asylum seekers or recent immigrants, when actually this was a 'home grown' problem involving young British Muslims[13].

Thus, the crucial factor that was sometimes ignored in the debate on asylum and immigration was that most of the suspected bombers, linked both to July 7, 2005 as well as July 21, 2005 , were actually British citizens. Obviously, deportation or other methods of control became more complicated if the authorities were dealing with UK citizens. Discussions on introducing anti-terror legislation and similar laws took place on all news channels and this will be analysed below.

The debate on asylum also served to make the connection between terrorist activities in the UK and overseas influences, that is, the global terrorist movement. This was another pertinent theme in most news coverage and will also be explored.

LOYALTY AND BELONGING

All channels identified the phenomenon of young British men choosing to participate in such acts of terror against their fellow citizens. The ITV and BBC news used basic discourses of fear, incompatibility, difference, loyalty and trust in presenting arguments about why these men were choosing to give up their 'normal' lives and sacrifice everything in such a manner. By describing the young men as having had a normal upbringing, education, job, family and living ordinary lives, until their (re)discovery of Islam, the reports focused on Islam as being the main factor that had lead them away from this normality into something extreme and sinister. They had now become the enemy within (Ansari, 2004). In fact this purported that *any* Muslim, especially a young male – ordinary as they seem – had the potential to become a recruit for this type of extreme activity.

Only news reports on C4 and on the Newsnight programme went on to analyse in some detail the possibilities of why this was happening. That is not to say they too did not employ discourses of difference and 'otherness' but they took the viewer into a deeper understanding of the reasons for the frustration and alienation that may possibly be driving young Muslims to such extremes. They presented both national issues of concern – such as deprivation and marginalisation, as well as international dimensions relating directly to British foreign policy, most recently the war in Iraq and looked at how being disenfranchised from the mainstream – socially, culturally and politically – meant people felt compelled to take such drastic measures. C4 also looked at the possible role of propaganda by political organisations such as *Al-Muhajiroun* in the recruitment of young men who were then encouraged to translate their political beliefs and grievances into physical action such as the bombings.

---

[13]

Shami Chakarbati, Director of Liberty, speaking on BBC 'Have Your Say – Questions of Security', July 2005.

The discourse of loyalty and belonging is a familiar one that was frequently articulated after September 2001, not only with reference to Muslims in the USA but all Muslims living in the West. Subsequently, after the July bombings the same kinds of questions were being asked of Muslims living in Britain. So whilst asylum seekers were seen as problematic and potentially dangerous because of their inherent 'Otherness' and thus evidently dissimilar values, British Muslims were seen as holding latent disaffection from the country of their birth and upbringing. When it came to the moment of truth, their opinions and actions would reflect more accurately the values of some other universal value system (that is, their religion and all that it implies) rather than what could be expected from the majority of citizens in the UK. The discovery that the perpetrators were British merely confirmed for some commentators what they had already suggested for some time, the conflict between the British way of life and values and belonging to the global Muslim community – the *ummah*, especially in its political manifestations.

C4 and Newsnight investigated the debates relating to British Muslims in special reports, whilst ITV and BBC news only touched on the issue of the Muslim community in Britain. Issues relating to the role of mosques, Muslim/non-Muslim relations, identity, integration/assimilation, local/national government perceptions and responses and police relations were all explored in the more detailed reports. The idea that a young British Muslim man could blow up not only himself but also innocent people, who were also fellow citizens, was something which caused great consternation amongst all observers. Suicide bombing on British soil marked a watershed in the threat of terrorism. Violent behaviour and political activism had always been the province of people 'out there', in the Middle East and in countries suffering from political turmoil, but now this type of insurgency and violence had begun here in the UK. Apart from the obvious dismay this caused, it also had far reaching implications for the way the terrorist threat would be policed and how related intelligence would be sought.

Again, if we use Poole's ideas of topical clusters, the above discourses on British-ness, 'Otherness', loyalty, belonging etc can fit into an overarching theme of integration and assimilation and 'threat to values' (Poole, 2002. p. 260). These ideas are obviously debated in relation to all minority populations, but particularly Muslims. Arguably this stems from the historical assumptions that Islam is not compatible with Christianity or Europe or the West or its modern secular principles. As a result of this, even if Muslims were born and grew up in Britain and even display all the visible signifiers of British youth culture, there is something intrinsic to their constitution that makes them inherently 'different' and the Other. No number of external reference points can change the basic fact that they will always remain different. It is this difference that results in any Muslim being seen as a potential danger, capable of perpetrating such acts of terror.

The media often makes a distinction between the acts of extreme Muslims and the beliefs and actions of 'mainstream' or 'moderate' Muslims. Reporting of the July bombings was no exception. Britain's Muslim communities were presented as law abiding people who did not condone such acts of terror and such radical ideologies were attributed to an extreme fringe that is in the minority and mainly unacceptable to other Muslims. However with the above discourses, describing Muslims as having a *potential* to develop such extreme views and behaviour regardless of their moderate standing, differentiating between different types of Muslims can prove to be ineffective. The overall impact means viewers' perceptions of Muslims and especially of Islam will inevitably deteriorate. The filtering of 'good' and 'bad' Muslims did not necessarily have the desired impact or outcomes as far as audience reception is concerned.

GLOBAL DIMENSIONS AND GEOPOLITICS

Tying in closely to this idea of dual loyalty or untrustworthiness is the idea that Muslims form part of a wider global network of ideologies and aspirations. These global connections were analysed by all of the news programmes, to a greater or lesser degree.

One of the findings of research looking at media coverage of Islam and Muslims is that a substantial proportion of the news material has an international dimension (Said, 1996). Reporting on wars, conflicts, diplomatic incidents, disasters and 'unusual' news relating to Muslims abroad outweighs local and national news stories (Poole, 2002). Thus, whilst the focus of the London bombings was the UK, links between overseas Muslims and groups were made and Islam was presented as a global force. Global terror networks were invoked as well as terror cells developing and operating within the UK.

Table 3:	Terror and Global Dimensions			
	BBC	Newsnight	ITV	C4
Terror Cells	5	6	1	1
Global Links/FP	3	8	2	3
Countries	6	4	15	9

FP – Foreign Policy. Countries – Only Muslim countries

All of the news programmes talked about 'terror cells', though ITV and C4 did so to a lesser extent (see Table 3). In connecting overseas cells with those in the UK, comparisons were made between the bombings here and other attacks abroad. The incidents in Kenya, Bali, Turkey and Egypt[14] were some of the examples used by way of reminding the viewer of the kinds of dangers posed by extreme groups. One important factor in referring to this global connection was the role of Al-Qaeda. Al-Qaeda[15] was the elusive entity that was invoked to explain previous attacks, most significantly on 9/11, and seen as having a role in influencing, if not actually carrying out, the July bombings. The attacks on the USA made an obvious point of comparison and the idea that terrorists were targeting powerful western nations was confirmed by other attacks in Paris and Madrid – London being the latest victim[16].

---

[14] A bomb exploded in July 2005 after the London bombing, but earlier incidents were also mentioned.

[15] Not mentioned explicitly by BBC news.

[16] All news programmes mentioned 9/11, though only ITV talked about the Paris and Madrid bombs.

Table 4:	Al-Qaeda and Osama bin Laden			
	BBC	Newsnight	ITV	C4
Al-Qaeda	-	10	2	5
Osama bin Laden	-	5	1	3

Connected with Al-Qaeda was the name of Osama bin Laden (OBL), which was cited by three of the four news programmes (see Table 4), when trying to analyse the motives behind the July attacks. His stance on western foreign policy towards Muslim countries, particularly that of the USA but also of the UK and other Western nations, was cited as an explanation of why many Muslims felt disillusioned with certain governments and policies. As such the role of foreign policy was discussed directly by the news programmes (though surprisingly, to a lesser degree by the BBC). The war in Iraq, including the decision to go to war; the reality of the situation there; long term policy, and, the actual impact of the continuing occupation by foreign forces, were all points of discussion with respect to recent foreign policies. However, a deeper understanding of the politics of the region, namely the Israeli-Palestinian conflict and specifically the role of Western nations in this, was almost completely absent from news reports. Considerable research has been done on the media coverage of the Middle Eastern situation, with a number of reports showing that there is bias towards the Israeli perspective at the expense of the Palestinian points of view and that fairness in reporting is often compromised (Greg & Berry, 2004).

A study by the Glasgow University Media Group shows the effect of this on public understanding. The key findings are summarised below:

- 82% of people listed TV news as their source of information.
- 80% of viewers did not know where the Palestinian refugees had come from and how they had become refugees.
- Of 3,536 lines of news bulletin text, only 17 explained the history of the conflict.
- The key issue of water is barely mentioned.
- 71% of viewers did not know that it was the Israelis who were occupying the territories.
- 9% of viewers knew that it was the Israelis who were occupying and that the settlers were Israeli.
- 11% of viewers believed that the Palestinians were occupying the territories and that the settlers were Palestinian.
- Palestinian bombings were frequently presented as "starting" a sequence of events which provoked an Israeli "response".
- Words such as "murder", "atrocity", "lynching" and "savage cold-blooded killing" were used only to describe Israeli deaths.
- Only 30% of viewers believed that more Palestinians had died than Israelis.

The BBC launched an inquiry into allegations of bias in its reporting of the Palestinian – Israeli issue, and whilst not finding itself to be biased, took measures to ensure that more context is explained, notably by appointing veteran journalist Jeremy Bowen as a senior correspondent in the area to provide context to reports from the conflict in addition to pieces filed by other reporters (BBC, Tuesday, 22 June, 2004).

Providing context in the reporting of any event is imperative, but particularly so in the case of sensitive or critical events such as the London bombings. Though the news programmes talked about related issues, they did not concentrate enough on presenting broader historical and political arguments that were being articulated by different voices, especially Muslim voices. Indeed it was not only 'Islamist' voices but those from various political perspectives which considered that wider debates and issues needed to be understood and resolved. Only then can there be a move towards eliminating, or at least reducing, the factors that motivate these terrorist attacks. Newsnight's feature, in which two Muslim spokespeople and another academic commentator were interviewed, was one example of efforts made by the programmes in this regard[17].

Though wider debate and context has been found to be lacking in news reporting of many issues (Conte, 2001), it would not have been difficult to provide this in the case of the bombings because all the programmes gave continuous coverage of the event for several weeks. If more time had been dedicated to developing a body of knowledge around the topics relating to the bombings, the audience may have been able to better understand the wider issues of concern and perhaps even be presented with alternative perspectives. The BBC bulletins were particularly restrictive and repetitive in their reporting and did not appear to investigate outside a fixed set of notions, whereas C4 and Newsnight at least enabled varied discussions and interviewed representatives of different organisations and standpoints which assisted audiences in constructing a broader framework within which to locate the bombings. The analysis charts for both BBC and ITV news show that similar words and phrases were used by both programmes in their overall reporting[18]. ITV's report on East Africa allowed them to mention country names linked to this region, which was not apparent in the BBC bulletins. It would appear that for both the BBC and ITV there were a very limited number of reports, if any, referring to 'socio-cultural' descriptions or explanations, which were found in the other two news programmes.

Apart from the obvious mention of Iraq in news programmes, other countries were also referred to, including, Afghanistan, Pakistan, Saudi Arabia, Somalia and other east African countries. The actual debate around foreign policy issues was on the whole limited. Whilst the war in Iraq was cited several times as being a reason for the attacks, this did not portray the full extent to which global political situations in the Muslim world were impacting on the perceptions of Muslims about western governments.

From the above analysis it can be seen that media, in this case television news continues to represent Islam and Muslims in a way that sees them as problematic and threatening. By using disparaging language and discourses which connote difference and incompatibility, the presence of Muslims in Britain (and in the West in general) is constructed as 'foreign' and potentially dangerous. Although these discourses were easily articulated in relation to the London bombings, other underlying assumptions which are known to be Islamophobic (for example, inferiority, backwardness or disloyalty) continue to circulate in the language and content of mainstream media.

---

[17] Farena Alam, editor of *Q-News*, Faisal Bodi, commentator for The Guardian, and Ted Cantle were interviewed on 30 July 2005.

[18] However, it must be noted that a substantial data set was missing for ITV news, so it cannot be said for certain that they did not explore more diverse issues.

One of the criticisms of reporting on Islam and Muslims in the media is that this takes place within a limited framework (Richardson, 2001). Only a selected number of topics, key words and perspectives are associated with Islam and these are used repeatedly, both in electronic and print media.

Previous research has shown that Muslims feel the media is one of the main factors which cause social discrimination and misunderstanding between themselves and the rest of society (Ameli *et al*, 2004a, 2004b, 2005, 2006a). Media was also identified as one of the specific reasons that leads Muslims to feel either neutral or negative about being affiliated with the UK and hence made them question the idea of equal citizenship and belonging (Ameli & Merali, 2004). In the same study, when asked what their expectations of the government were, they stated that 'eliminating Islamophobia and the demonisation of Muslims' was a major priority for the government. Much of the creation and perpetuation of Islamophobic attitudes was blamed on the media and it was felt that unless the government checked the media for their portrayal, it would only lead to the reinforcing of negative attitudes towards Muslims. These negative attitudes were seen as directly impacting on the experiences of social discrimination amongst Britain's Muslim communities. Further research with regard to these questions was carried out for this volume and will be referred to later on. Notably, however the analysis of TV News, even where 'all good intentions' were exhibited (Shadjareh, quoted in Ansari, 2005), shows a limited framework within which Muslims and Islam were discussed. This in turn evidenced a control on discourse by the majority, and the participation of Muslims on the terms set out for them, rather than in a way which is meaningful for them, resulting in the muting of Muslims as a minority. The prevalence of domination in the discourse produced demonisation regardless of intention, and this is of great significance in that demonisation as an ideology no longer needs to be the result of a conspiracy or project or the accumulation of deliberate malice – domination of the majority now necessarily means demonisation of the minority Other.

THE BIG SCREEN - MUSLIM REPRESENTATION IN CINEMA

This section looks at the role of cinema in representations of Islam, Muslims and Arabs by examining a selection of films.

Whilst news media can be clearly identified as representing 'reality', the big screen occupies a more ambiguous position as source of 'truth'. Film and cinema are a great source of cultural awareness and information but whilst they are mainly, and quite obviously, fictional, the impact of film discourse cannot be underestimated. This is particularly the case when storylines and genres relate to actual events or are set in frameworks of understanding that have relevance to real life. So for example, when films refer to actual events or engage in existing political debates, their role as social and cultural critic begins to develop.

For this analysis, a range of film genres were examined, including action thrillers (*The Siege*: 1998, *Executive Decision*: 1996), drama (*House of Sand and Fog*: 2003, *East is East*: 1999) and children's cartoons (*Aladdin*: 1992), for their representation of Islam, Muslims and Arabs. It was evident from all genres that they contained negative stereotypes about Islam and Muslims/ Arabs. The thrust of these differed as did the actual manifestation, nevertheless, they all exhibited examples of Islamophobic discourses. Thus a broad spectrum including Hollywood action blockbusters, cartoons and British artistic movies are all means through which either crude or exaggerated stereotypes are reinforced or otherwise more subtle disdain of Islam is obtained.

CINEMATIC ISLAMOPHOBIA

The action movie genre is more overtly – and perhaps more easily – able to focus on topics such as threat, violence, fear and terrorism and this was the case in both *The Siege* (1998) and *Executive Decision* (1994). Here there is greater opportunity to represent conflict, tension, physical combat and so on and there appeared to be less need to use subtle discourses and references. Both of these films were criticised by the Muslim community for the stereotypical 'clash of civilisations' theory and negative portrayal of Islam and Muslims / Arabs, depicting them as the enemy. This enemy constituted not only a foreign threat but was also illustrated as the 'enemy within' – Arab American citizens. In the case of less apparent Islamophobia in films, whilst they may appear innocent or harmless, they may in fact have a more detrimental effect on people's perceptions of Islam and Muslims because they function to reinforce 'acceptable' prejudice of another religion or culture (Hall, 1993).

Film: The Siege
Year: 1998
Genre: Action
Director: Edward Zwick
Screenwriter: Lawrence Wright

Main Actors: Tony Shalboub, Annette Bening, Denzel Washington and Bruce Willis

Brief Summary: As a response to an Islamic religious leader's abduction by the US military, New York City experiences an increase in terrorist attacks. Anthony Hubbard, the head of the FBI's Counter-Intelligence Task Force teams up with CIA operative Elise Kraft to hunt for those responsible for the attacks, only to find that Elise's partner, the last terrorist cell, is planning to suicide bomb a protest demanding equality for Arabs. Meanwhile, when the President declares martial law, General William Devereaux arrests Arab-American males, imprisons them in an open air stadium and makes plans to torture and kill them.

Main Characters
Denzel Washington	Anthony 'Hub' Hubbard
Annette Bening	Elise Kraft/Sharon Bridger
Bruce Willis	Major General William Devereaux
Tony Shalhoub	Agent Frank Haddad

The Siege, as its title suggests, centres on the 'invasion' of New York City by Palestinian terrorists. Released three years prior to the bombing of the twin towers, the film sets out an expectation of Muslim perpetrated terrorism on the streets of New York. The terrorists randomly target innocent New Yorkers, on buses, in schools, on the street, in order to cause mayhem and strike fear in the hearts of the public and administration alike, and are all human / suicide bombers. Set as this was at a time when no human / suicide bombings had been perpetrated in a Western country, the impact of this representation is important in quelling suggestions that Islamophobic or prejudicial representation of Muslims as terrorists and potential suicide bombers is a 'natural' result of atrocities like the Madrid and London bombings, and one that negates the rights of Muslims to complain.

In the film, Arab immigrants as well as Arab Americans are shown to be amongst the network of cells of terrorists, implying that the threat is global but with 'home' links. This kind of theme has profound implications for the status and position of Arab American citizens in the eyes of their fellow Americans as well as having an impact on the way Muslims and Arabs worldwide are viewed. The overseas element of the network – Palestine – is not portrayed in its fuller context, though mention is made of 'tensions' in the 'Middle East' and Iraq is referred to on several occasions.

The close relationship between reality and film stories (Andrew, 1984) is apparent in *The Siege* on a number of occasions. Use of stock (real life) footage of burning buildings and responses from the White House are intertwined with the story, so whilst showing a real fire in Lebanon, we are told that 'terrorists' attacked a US army barracks. Also when referring to another attack in the film, news reporters tell us that 'this is the worst attack on US soil since the Oklahoma City bomb' – blurring fiction with factual incidents that had a very particular impact on the USA.

This is perhaps one of the greatest concerns for such movies as they portray everyday scenes familiar to audiences – New York sidewalks, neighbourhoods, the skyline, taxis, Broadway, etc – and then transpose upon them potential terrorist attacks, untrustworthy Arabs, dangerous foreign immigrants and so on. The film brings into focus some of the worst American fears, that is, Muslims or Arabs attacking the country; murdering men, women and children; causing wanton destruction; wreaking havoc to the peaceful and systematic lives of citizens; and, 'attacking our way of life' (as a US chief of staff is quoted as saying in the film). Demonisation in this film has clearly preceded real life events, but key elements make the film's representation even more alarming.

Apart from the monolithic stereotype of the Arab/Palestinian/Muslim being violent and ready to be martyred for their cause (a 'cause' which is never given any context and seems puzzling to the average American), a considerable number of other stereotypes about the Muslim/Arab culture and religion were presented in the film. Muslim men are shown praying in a mosque, a call to prayer is made from a New York mosque minaret, recitation of the Quran or prayers are said in Arabic and one of the 'mastermind' terrorists is shown using a rosary. All of these scenes are dotted about in the film between acts of violence, bombs exploding and indiscriminate killing, and more often than not they have no direct connection to the overall storyline. Thus Islamic ritual practices are shown in close succession with scenes of unacceptable behaviour and locate Muslims in the broader context of violence, disloyalty and untrustworthiness implying that terrorist acts are intrinsic to Islamic belief and practice.

Controversy before the film was released centred on the movie trailer aired in cinemas, where the inter-cutting of Islamic ritual and terroristic violence featured heavily. The film's star Denzel Washington also came out to criticise the trailer in that it 'misrepresented' what the film was talking about. Supporters of the film suggested that it intended (with some justification) to relate the possibilities of military extremism (internment, torture and murder of suspects etc.) on American soil in the face of a terrorist threat which would ultimately negate the civil liberties that 'America stands for'. Much mention is made in the film of American complicity in setting up and assisting 'extremist' groups in the Middle East – a concern that has featured in the writings of many (American) left-wing writers e.g. Noam Chomsky, and which is an unusual source for the Hollywood mainstream. Indeed one of the main characters 'Sharon' becomes involved in the investigation as a way of expiating her guilt in this process of 'teaching' cells in the Middle East, the tricks of the trade. She also tries to help investigators differentiate between 'good' Muslims / Arabs – those who may be politically militant but are ultimately secularised and pose no terrorist threat e.g. her boyfriend, a Palestinian lecturer who holds and passes key information on 'extremists' to the authorities.

The argument that this film is a rallying cry for societal unity in the face of dual threats of military extremism and international Islamist terrorism is strengthened both by the subtle but essentially unsympathetic portrayal of General Devereaux (Bruce Willis) whose implication in the abduction of an Arab cleric who is also a militant leader, spurs the chain of events that lead his supporters to commit acts of terrorism in the USA. Devereaux not only denies the abduction and is seen to have the cleric in custody, he also manipulates the acts of terrorism to have military law imposed on New York. He is shown as a torturer, and ultimately, murderer who justifies his actions on the extremes of the situation. He is eventually seen to be arrested by Hub (Washington) and military law lifted.

The end of the film depicts Muslims / Arabs and non-Muslims walking off into the distance as one community, once military law is lifted, and follows a long denouement which involves the uncovering of the final terrorist plot to blow up a civil rights rally of Muslims and non-Muslims protesting at internment.

The film's heroes Hub and Sharon uncover this plot and are assisted by Sharon's boyfriend who states he will help them find the last bomber about whom he has information and will even help to mediate between him and them in an attempt to avert the tragedy. This 'differentiation' between good and bad Muslim, secular and Islamic, educated and rural, activist and terrorist is the enduring narrative and reinforces an ethnocentric discourse of us and them as well as defining the level of accessibility of what constitutes a good Muslim / Arab American. This is itself unsubtle, stereotypical and demonising and implies that religiosity and anything more than a cultural or formalistic attachment to specifically the Islamic faith is dangerous and subversive to 'American' values, reemphasising the theories of domination – Islam is backward, illiberal and dangerous and so by dint, confessing Muslims must be so too.

Beyond this however is a further act of demonisation that undermines the film's claims to set out a broadly liberal stall, and that is the betrayal of Samir, Sharon's boyfriend, the secular Palestinian activist and informant. Creating a diversion where Hub gets lost he takes Sharon to an empty Turkish baths where Sharon is expecting a meeting with the final suicide bomber. As her boyfriend starts taking ritual ablution, Sharon realises to her horror that her boyfriend is in fact the last bomber and that all along he has been using her. His invective at this point imbues all the lack of sophistication of a Bond villain monologue, where he announces his enmity to the USA based on their betrayal of the cause they helped fund and create (implicitly a vague pan-Palestinian, Iraqi Islamic militancy). In his eyes the final insult was the kidnapping of a cleric 'a holy man' as he states, a crime for which innocent Americans must pay. Hub is able to locate the pair and due to Sharon's heroism and self-sacrifice the bombing is stopped (Sharon is killed in the process). Effectively even a 'good' Muslim in this context could well be a 'religious, irrational, terrorist' in disguise, and this final scene exemplifies all that is bad about the Muslim / Arab - he is promiscuous, treacherous, untrustworthy, violent, cold-blooded, has contempt for his victims, ruthless and yet willing to give his own life. Ultimately Samir's secular anger at America hitherto represented as acceptable dissent was a signifier of potential danger. As the only voice of dissent that was not initially represented as terroristic, his ultimate portrayal undermines the plurality of voices in the film.

Sharon's complexity, education and loyalty are posited in sharp contrast to another easily identifiable cultural stereotype i.e. the veiled women who permeate the film as wives of key characters devoid of any character or background figures that form part of the landscape of an Arabised Brooklyn. There is some ambiguous suggestion at the end of the film that Sharon may herself have been a secret Muslim, as Hub attempts to give her the last rites as she lies dying, the last words she says as he dies are in Arabic and refer to 'Allah'. Yet again, however this posits Sharon in the role of (possible) 'good' Muslim – one who is not only unveiled but scantily clad, appears in a nude scene, is in an extramarital relationship and is ultimately ready to sacrifice herself for America against a(nother) Muslim. The film is replete with characters that portray 'Muslim citizenship' in a western context as conditional upon 'extra' and unquestioning loyalty to the state, even when that state is supposed to imbue the value of dissent and pluralism. This is a concern that is mirrored in the real life understandings of Muslims as regards public discourse on Muslims and citizenship (Ameli et al 2004a, 2004b, and 2006b) and its prevalence in fictional representation cannot be underestimated.

Other stereotypes include men with beards, men wearing Arab dress, food shops and stalls and Arabic posters were all depicted in a Brooklyn neighbourhood. Arabic is spoken on several occasions and Arab music also plays in the background in several scenes. At one point when martial law is declared in Brooklyn (an odd notion in itself but perhaps not considered impossible by some members of the audience) all Arab and Middle Eastern men are rounded up and interned in a sports stadium. Here many are shown as having dark complexions, often unshaven, wearing traditional Arab hats and clothes and wandering around in groups. As Said (1996) states, the Arab is often shown in a mass – nameless, faceless, stripped of any individuality that would enable the viewer to make that human connection with him as a person with experiences similar to anyone else. Similarly the female members of the families of these men are shown as crowds waiting for the release of their fathers, brothers or sons.

To gain a better understanding of the international context that the film is trying to portray, it is useful to simply list all the countries mentioned and 'implicated' in the network of nations bent on organising terror against the USA. Palestine (the *Intifada*), Israel, Iraq (Gulf War), Lebanon (Beirut), Saudi Arabia, 'The Middle East', Afghanistan, Iran, Libya, Syria, Somalia, and somewhat surprisingly Russia and Haiti. The terrorists are mentioned as having already attacked Israel, Lebanon and Saudi Arabia before moving on to the USA. The spectre of foreign terrorism is described as coming to US soil – a fear which no doubt exists in the minds of American people in reality. "Beirut came to Brooklyn today" quips one of the newsreaders as scenes of a blown up bus are shown on news reports across the country. Furthermore the threat of 'foreign' terrorism is played out in two ways – immigration and Arab Americans. The former is referred to through references to INS, immigration control, unknown numbers of Arabs and people from the Middle East entering the USA and the usual 'we are being swamped' scenarios which are not unfamiliar in the UK. More worrying is the implication that the latter, Arab American citizens, are too part of this conspiracy to bring the country to its knees, simply by virtue of their inherent 'otherness'. Again this is not an unfamiliar trope used against Muslims in Britain or the West in general. Regardless of legal status and citizenship, and perhaps having lived in the country for over half a century, the otherness of Muslims is still evident. From

Brooklyn car mechanics to college lecturers and all Arab immigrants, the monolithic portrayal of Arabs as terrorists vilified a whole culture and people, adding to the already existing negativity and hostility faced by Muslims.

ARAB AND ISLAM AS A SYMBOL OF VIOLENCE

Film: Executive Decision
Year: 1996
Genre: Action/ Thriller
Director: Stuart Baird
Screenwriter: Jim Thomas & John Thomas

Main Actors: Kurt Russell, Steven Seagal Halle Berry

Brief Summary: When a Boeing 747 is hijacked by terrorists, an American intelligence expert believes that their plan is to launch a nerve gas attack on Washington DC rather than air piracy. The US government, ignoring the agent's nerve gas theory is left with two choices; to shoot down the plane killing all 400 passengers or to let it land. However Colonel Travis and his counter terrorism team decide to board the plane using a special aircraft to save the day.

Main Characters
Kurt Russell	Dr. Phil David Grant
Steven Seagal	Lt. Colonel Austin Travis
Halle Berry	Jean, Flight Attendant

Similarly in *Executive Decision* the audience is confronted with yet another set of Palestinian terrorists. Having hijacked a Boeing 747, they proceed to beat and kill innocent people, including an air hostess and a US senator (who was about to enter into negotiations for them), en-route to blowing up Washington, DC and the Eastern Seaboard of the USA with barrels of a nerve gas (DZ-5). In the opening scene, US soldiers raid a house where the DZ-5 is thought to have been kept after having been stolen by Chechens. Later, a well-known terrorist, Jaffa El-Sayed, is hijacked and then handed to the US so that he can be used as a bargaining chip by his own second in command, Nagi Hassan, played by David Suchet.

Nagi, sporting an Arab accent, on several occasions prays or makes reference to Allah or Islam, even saying *Allahu Akbar* with his last breath as he is shot dead aboard the plane. His conversation with Jaffa captures some of the most inaccurate and damaging associations made with Islam and Muslims:

"Rejoice in your freedom,
Allah has blessed us.
A great destiny awaits us both,
All of Islam will embrace you as its leader.
I am your flame,
The sword of Allah,
And with it I will strike deep into the heart of the infidel".

On hearing of Jaffa's release the other hijackers cheer – shouting *Allahu Akbar* as they think their mission has been successful, unaware that Nagi's grand plan is to blow up the USA and not secure the release of Jaffa. When Nagi's co-hijacker asks Nagi why they are not rerouting to Algeria as was the original plan, he continues:

"Allah has chosen for us a task greater than Jaffa's freedom. We are the true soldiers of Islam. Our destiny is to deliver the vengeance of Allah into the belly of the infidel".

His comrade responds, "This is not Allah's will" and is swiftly shot dead for expressing his dissent and daring to undermine the grand plan. The others are subdued and return to their positions.

Similar to *The Siege, Executive Decision*, plays on the worst fears of Americans (and indeed other Westerners to a degree) about suicide bombers, hatred towards the USA (though this is always presented as a jealously or unfounded hatred rather than contextualised in the wider debates of global politics), about a potential terrorist lurking in every Arab/Middle Eastern/Muslim looking person, and the incompatibility of Islamic and Western values and cultures. The terrorists in both films show a blatant disregard for innocent lives, not flinching whilst killing men, women, children, elderly or vulnerable people – indeed this is one of the most malicious and virulent stereotypes of Muslims (Shaheen, 2003). The terrorists in both films are shown as partaking in religious rituals, particularly reciting prayers and reading or referring to the Quran – even erroneously defending their actions by it. In the case of Nagi, he makes a point of praying/reciting before and after killing someone. Therefore equating Islamic practices with acts of terrorism, indeed almost defining 'terrorism' as an Islamic ritual is evident. This is indeed a false and dangerous assumption. Further fear and hostility towards the Middle East and Muslims is emphasised by referring to a number of countries including Palestine, Iraq, Chechnya, Algeria and also the Gulf War.

Various commentators have expressed concern that Hollywood villains are frequently turning out to be Palestinians (see Shaheen, 2003). No real context is presented to the Israeli-Palestinian conflict and the generally negative views towards Arabs and Islam in the USA are further reinforced through cinematic propaganda. Shaheen (2003) notes that this is especially the case when producers have a 'political agenda' and when many of the films are 'made-in-Israel':

> "Dictating numerous Palestinian-as-terrorist scenarios is the Israeli connection. More than half (28) of the Palestinian movies were filmed in Israel. Nearly all of the made-in-Israel films, especially the Cannon[19] movies, display violent, sex-crazed Palestinian 'bastards and animals' contesting Westerners, Israelis and fellow Arabs. I believe Cannon's poisonous scenarios are not accidental, but rather propaganda disguised as entertainment" (p 27).

It is important therefore to stress the potential that films have of propagating particular ideological discourses and representing political ideas to mass audiences. The power of the big screen is not just exercised to audiences in the USA, indeed one of the biggest exports of the country is perhaps Hollywood 'entertainment'. The question that is asked time and again is whether such disparaging ideas would be acceptable of any other ethnic or religious group.

The cultural stereotypes and scenarios are patently obvious in *Raiders of the Lost Ark* as most of it is set in Egypt (though actually filmed in Tunisia). On arriving in Cairo, Indiana Jones and his fearless female companion, Marion, visit the home of Jones' sidekick, Sallah. They are served by his wife, who dressed in black, passively moves about looking after her husband's guests and generally being the good wife and hostess.

Film: Raiders of the Lost Ark
Year: 1981
Genre: Action/Adventure
Director: Steven Spielberg
Screenwriter: George Lucas & Phillip Kaufman

Main Actors: Harrison Ford, Karen Allen, Paul Freeman, Ronald Lacey and Johnathan Rhys-Davies

Brief Summary: Indiana Jones, an archaeologist, is employed by the US government to find the powerful Ark of the Covenant before the Nazis lay their hands on it.

Main Characters:
Harrison Ford	Indiana Jones
Karen Allen	Marion Ravenwood
Paul Freeman	Dr. Rene Belloq
Ronald Lacey	Major Toht
John Rhys-Davies	Sallah

In contrast, representing the Western woman is Marion, an independent, spirited and brave traveller. A little later, a street scene again embodies further stereotypes of what the filmmakers want to show us of Cairo and by extension, the Arab world – veiled women, bearded men in traditional dress, bazaars, fruit stalls, hats, drinking vessels, cobbled pavements, narrow streets, sandy and rough surroundings and old architecture. All of these are shown with a backdrop of snake-charming music, interrupted only by the call to prayer. In a café, men sit drinking tea and smoking water pipes, whilst beggars run up to Jones hassling him for '*bakshish*'.

At the scene of the archaeological dig, we see faceless groups of Arab men dressed in traditional *abayahs*, singing in Arabic or reciting as they work. Palm trees, camels and tents all direct the viewer to the things typically associated with Arab cultures and places. The film characterises good and bad Arabs – basically divided into those on Indiana Jones' side and those working for the Nazis. The Egyptians are shown as labourers at the dig, street vendors or beggars, and those fighting against Jones are shown as brutish and violent thugs. The popularity of the Indiana Jones series, a huge box office success, meant that it was no doubt watched by millions worldwide, and for a long time, the first movie in the series, held the position of one of the most watched movies of all time. It must undoubtedly have had an impact on ideas and images of Arabs and Egyptians amongst both young and old cinema-goers.

RACISM, ISLAMOPHOBIA OR BOTH?

House of Sand and Fog tells the story of an Iranian family living in the USA who become involved in a dispute with a young woman over the ownership of a seafront house. After the county repossesses the house from the young woman, the Iranian family become its legal owners by purchasing it at an auction. The objective of the Iranian man, Colonel Massoud Amir Behrani, is to use this as a stepping stone to acquiring their dream home that will be similar to their home on the Caspian Sea in Iran. This home had held many happy memories for them until they were forced to flee Iran following the Islamic Revolution in 1979. At the wedding ceremony of his daughter, Behrani reminds his guests how the "*Ayatollah*s ripped the soul out of our beautiful country" and constructs in the imagination of the viewer the common and negative description of the Revolution, without enabling any detailed or balanced analysis of the event. The Iranian guests are shown as drinking alcohol, dancing, wearing Western clothes and generally as 'secular' Iranians.

> **Film: House of Sand and Fog**
> **Year:** 2003
> **Genre:** Drama
> **Director:** Vadim Perelman
>
> **Screenwriter:** Vadim Perelman & Shawn Lawrence Otto
>
> **Main Actors:** Jennifer Connelly and Ben Kingsley
>
> **Brief Summary:** Kathy, an abandoned wife, finds herself wrongly evicted from her home and embroiled in a battle with the new Iranian owners of her home.
>
> **Main Characters**
> Jennifer Connelly — Kathy
> Ben Kingsley — Massoud Amir Behrani

This one line contextualises for the audience an immensely complex set of social, political, cultural and religious developments in a country that Said (1996) argues has come to be known to Americans through the hostage taking crisis and the overthrow of the Shah. All the negativity associated with the Islamic Revolution, indeed with Islam, is recalled and confirmed by this statement. Though Behrani is shown as a hardworking man whose principle objective is to look after his family, his character is somewhat ambiguous. He is repeatedly shown as being violent towards his wife, Nadia, as well as the young woman to whom the house belonged. Conversely, when she tries to kill herself he brings her to his house and the whole family looks after her. Nadia is shown as a passive and 'good wife' – "I will do as you wish" – she subserviently replies to Behrani in one scene, though she too is shown as being passionate and emotional in one or two scenes where she has an outburst against her husband. "Have you no respect for me or faith in me?" Behrani asks her, before proceeding to slap her across the face when she continues shouting at him. This stereotype of the Muslim man as a 'wife-beater' is reinforced on several occasions. Whilst he isn't the kind of 'Muslim' who backed the Revolution, he is nonetheless Muslim enough to be domineering and violent towards his wife.

Although a number of negative stereotypes are presented in the film there are arguably references to more positive aspects of Iranian culture and religion. Hospitable; family centred (in contrast to the police officer whose marriage is breaking down and is having an affair with the young woman, or indeed the woman herself whose husband has left her and whose brother is unwilling to come out to help her); and, hardworking (Behrani works as a builder and a garage sales assistant to meet his family's needs).

Reference to immigration/deportation is made by the police officer who visits Behrani in an attempt to scare him into re-selling the house back to the county. However, Behrani is confident and unperturbed by the threats whereas his wife becomes distraught at hearing they may be deported to Iran. She expresses her anxiety at how they and their children will be killed if they are forced to return.

On the whole, though Behrani's family acquired the house in a legal manner, they are not presented as the rightful owners, whereas we are encouraged to sympathise with the woman who is now homeless, sleeping in her car, having little or no money, washing in public places and struggling to right the wrong that has been done to her (though this 'wrong' was done by the county rather than Behrani). She tells how her father worked hard for 30 years to buy the house, which he left for her and her brother. Behrani's son Ismail, whose accent tells us he has been educated in the USA and is more American than his father, on a few occasions, expresses sympathy for the woman but his father reminds him that he needn't feel that way. Talking about her in particular and Americans in general he states, "She was not responsible, didn't pay her bills. They [Americans] do not deserve what they have, they are ungrateful. We are not like them; we don't throw away God's blessings". Behrani's explanation tends to strengthen the notion that Muslims have an aversion towards the West, and the USA in particular, and whilst they are somewhat jealous of their wealth and lifestyle, at the same time aspire to have the same. Muslims are depicted as ungrateful and despite their mimicry of Western ways, are ultimately averse to all Westerners. This replicates a central tenet of Samual Huntington's clash of civilisation theory in that non-Westerners (i.e. of ethnically and religiously non-White, and non-Christian heritage, whether based in the West or elsewhere) can only mimic but not comprehend European values which he suggests are unique not universal (Huntington, 1994). Without the universality of value, there is inherent and eternal backwardness, which Behrani represents. This is despite Behrani also representing a 'good' form of Muslim i.e. one that believes he would be killed if he returned to his 'Islamicised' homeland.

Later in the film, after the woman tries to kill herself, Behrani and his son are sitting down to eat and Behrani says that he too feels sorry for her. Nadia reminds Ismail that they have a guest in the house (after Behrani brings the woman in to save her life) and that he needs to be kind, polite, gentle and quiet. These instances appear to 'counter' the negative associations already established in the film. By the end of the film Nadia has begun to bond with the woman and she herself realises that Behrani is not buying her house simply to make money but for the future of his family. She appreciates their kindness and ultimately doesn't begrudge what has happened. In the concluding scene, when all 3 members of the Behrani family are dead (Ismail is shot by a police officer, after which Behrani kills his wife and then commits suicide) a police officer asks the woman if this is her house and she replies "no, this isn't my house".

The film sets up stereotypes about life in Iran before and after the Revolution, though no real information is actually given to the audience – it works on assumptions and prior understanding of the subject. It uses the 'taken for granted' assumptions that audiences have of life in Iran pre- and post-1979. Before there was the 'good life' but after people were forced to flee, opportunity was thwarted, restrictions were placed on personal freedom, religious laws were enforced and so on. It contrasted the American dream with the Iranian reality, that is, the ability to work hard and achieve what you want without being limited in any way as opposed to living in fear of your life. Nadia is shown to be very sensitive to the sight of blood, perhaps implying she has witnessed bloodshed in her home country. Overall though, whilst showing the human aspect of both sides, *House of Sand and Fog* presents some conventional stereotypes of Muslims and Iranians.

Even in *Return of the King* (the third part in the *Lord of the Rings* trilogy), which seems to have no obvious connection to Muslims or Islam, odd subtle references are made. For example, the Nazgul – evil birds – seem to have a Turkish or Iranian sounding name and huge elephant-like creatures carry black turban wearing enemies -blackened versions of Arabs on them during battle.

The British film *East it East* was much more crude and direct in its references to Pakistani culture and Islamic values. The film focuses on a family living in Greater Manchester in the 1970s. As the father is Pakistani and the mother English, it examines issues such as mixed marriage, children of mixed parentage, cultural adjustment, racism and inter-family conflict. Though many of the issues are indeed pertinent even today, it deals with these by using exaggerated stereotypes relating to language, dress, food, relationships and marriage, family, community, culture and religion. It deals with many serious aspects in a humorous way and this in some ways detracts from the gravity of issues such as domestic violence. However, the fact remains that the Muslim husband is shown as being both physically and verbally abusive to his wife.

> **Film: East is East**
> **Year: 1999**
> **Genre: Comedy/Drama**
> **Director: Damien O'Donnell**
> **Screenwriter: Ayub Khan-Din**
> **Main Actors:** Om Puri, Linda Bassett, Jordan Routledge, Archi Panjabi, Emil Marwa, Chris Bisson, Jimi Mistry and Raji James
>
> **Brief Summary:** A mixed-race, Anglo-Pakistani family, living in northern England in the early 1970s break loose from the traditional and cultural Pakistani background enforced upon them by their father.
>
> **Main Characters**
> | | |
> |---|---|
> | Om Puri | George Khan |
> | Linda Bassett | Ella Khan |
> | Jordan Routledge | Sajid Khan |
> | Archie Panjabi | Meenah Khan |
> | Emil Marwa | Maneer Khan |
> | Chris Bisson | Saleem Khan |
> | Jimi Mistry | Tariq Khan |
> | and Raji James | Abdul Khan |

The representation of George (the Anglicised version of Zaheed) as a Muslim husband, constantly referring to his 'first wife' in Pakistan; being domineering and aggressive, indeed physically violent; insisting his family adopt his values and way of life; expecting the children to be 'properly Pakistani'; choosing brides for his sons without consulting them, and; criticising English people and values, fits into many of the negative perceptions people have of Islam, Muslims and Pakistani culture. They include, amongst others, the 'four wives' question, the wife beater, the tyrant at home, unwilling to discuss things or consult children about their lives and forced marriages.

By portraying Islam as an alien religion and set of values which only George seems to be able to relate to, the children reject the centrality of it in their lives. Subsequently they hold little respect for its rules, so that when their father is at the mosque they eat sausages and bacon; have pre-marital relationships; Meena (the daughter) doesn't wear a veil or headscarf (apart from when the Imam tells her to); the oldest son is gay; they are not enthusiastic about learning the Quran at *madrasah*, and; they don't want to marry 'Pakis'. Only one of the sons is shown as praying and devout in his adherence to Islamic beliefs and practices and as a result he is given the nickname 'Gandhi'. Whilst the writer is portraying issues that he and others in a similar situation experienced when growing up in a mixed family, ultimately numerous references are made to Islam and Pakistani culture which are framed in a negative way.

Film: Aladdin
Year: 1992
Genre: Family Animation
Director: Ron Clements, John Musker
Screenwriter: Ted Elliot
Music/ Soundtrack: Alan Menken

Main Actors: Scott Weinger, Robin Williams, Linda Larkin, and Johnathan Freeman

Brief Summary: Aladdin, a streetwise young thief of Agrabah, falls in love with Princess Jasmine, the Sultan's daughter. The Sultan's Vizier, Jafar, deceives Aladdin into helping him acquire a magical lamp from the Cave of Wonders, which ends up in the hands of Aladdin. Genie, the lamp's occupant, grants Aladdin his wishes to become a prince and win the affections of Princess Jasmine. When Jafar finally steals the lamp back and gets three wishes of his own, Aladdin is left to use his own intelligence to topple Jafar and save Agrabah.

Main Characters
Scott Weinger	Aladdin 'Al'/ Prince Ali Ababwa (voice)
Robin Williams	Genie (voice)
Linda Larkin	Princess Jasmine (voice)
Jonathan Freeman	Grand Vizier Jafar (voice)

At possibly the other end of the spectrum of film genre are children's cartoons and although they seem innocent enough, Sardar (1998) amongst others, has demonstrated how in actual fact they duplicate and reinforce negative attitudes towards other people and cultures.

Sardar (1998) uses the example of *Pocahontas* to tease out the various scenarios used by producers such as 'good guys' and 'bad guys', superior and inferior cultures or justification of domination by Westerners and these concepts can be applied to other storylines. So for example in Walt Disney's *Aladdin*, the opening lines are sung by a storyteller travelling through the desert, mounted on a camel with the customary huge white turban, bulbous nose and beard.

"Oh I come from a land,
From a faraway place....
It's barbaric, but hey its home!"

Shaheen (2003) asks the question: why start a children's cartoon adventure with lyrics containing the word 'barbaric' and why describe a whole culture as such? In June 1993, in response to public pressure, Disney executives deleted two lines from the opening song:

"Where they cut off your ear
If they don't like your face"

It did however retain the line containing the word barbaric. The impression that this adjective leaves on the audience can be nothing but negative and derogatory. Throughout the film most of the Arab dwellers of '*Agrabah*' are shown as brutal, bumbling palace guards chasing Aladdin or maidens dressed in veils, street vendors or merchants selling their goods on market stalls. In contrast to the Arabs who are ruthless caricatures, Aladdin, Princess Jasmine and the Sultan are Anglicised (or Americanised to be precise) heroes of the film. They have American accents whilst the rest of the cast have exaggerated and ridiculous Arab accents. The genie even abbreviates Aladdin's name to 'Al' creating a more likeable character that the audience can relate to.

Rather than portray the Arab culture and Islamic religion in a positive or neutral light, the producers associate it with harsh punishments (wanting to cut off Princess Jasmine's hand because she gives a poor child an apple from one of the stalls without paying for it and Jafar saying that Aladdin has been beheaded); oppressive practices (the Sultan forcing Jasmine to marry a man of his choice against her wishes because that is the 'custom'); and, uncivilised or inferior cultural identifiers attributed to Islam (undeveloped market places, veiled women, harem maidens, villains, onion shaped domes, minarets, treasures, magic carpets, gold). Whilst many of the cultural symbols could be read as being positive or even neutral, the overall storyline creates a distinction between American culture and lifestyle and Arab culture and this is characterised by the different people. The former is shown as superior, eventually overcoming the latter.

American values are depicted through Aladdin and Jasmine – kindness to others, freedom, justice, humility and love, whereas the Arab culture is illustrated by the villains, including the evil vizier, Jafar who is barbaric, ruthless, sly, cruel, harsh and oppressive. The cartoon adventure, with its huge popularity amongst both young and old, offers a brilliant opportunity to challenge the hegemonic representations of the 'other' in mainstream television, cinema and other media, but more often than not this opportunity is missed. In fact animation could play a key role in determining ideas about different cultures and places at an early stage in people's lives.

Hollywood's' influence cannot be underestimated. After the initial screening at the cinema, these films are reproduced in various forms and circulate around the globe, reaching worldwide audiences in more than 100 countries. As Shaheen (2003, p. 9) notes:

> "Islam, particularly, comes in for unjust treatment. Today's image-makers regularly link the Islamic faith with male supremacy, holy war and acts of terror, depicting Arab Muslims as hostile alien intruders, and as lecherous, oily sheikhs intent on using nuclear weapons. When mosques are displayed on screen, the camera inevitably cuts to Arabs praying, and then gunning down civilians. Such scenarios are common fare."

It would seem that nothing has changed since Said (1981) described prevalent images of Arabs in almost the same words.

Similar to television news images and representations of Muslims and Islam, Shaheen (2003, p. 29) is in no doubt that the caricatures of the Arab in film have a considerable affect on all people, even influencing world public opinion and policy.

> "Not only do violent news images of extremists reinforce and exacerbate already prevalent stereotypes, but they serve as both a source and an excuse for continued Arab-bashing by those filmmakers eager to exploit the issue… Taken together, news and movie images wrench the truth out of shape to influence billions of people and regrettably, gross misperceptions abound".

With the resurgence of cinema in the 1990s, cinematic representation is of great importance in its impact on social psyche(s). The films discussed predate the terrorist attacks on America, Madrid and London, and if anything set up the expectation of such events many years in advance. They also emphasise, or arguably, cultivated, specific prejudices which have found open expression both in 'factual' media discourse and societal events (backlash violence and discrimination etc.) Muslim respondents in this project found a direct correlation between media portrayal and their social experiences of exclusion, hatred, discrimination and violence. Perhaps the most significant finding of the effect of the media, as perceived by Muslims, on the structural experience of Islamophobia by Muslims came from responses regarding education (see Ameli *et al*, 2005). Muslim school children, who had recounted in some detail the effects of alienation they felt from peers, teachers and a sense of marginalisation (not just by open hostility but through subtle means such as marginalisation from the curriculum and unintentional though prevalent Islamophobia) stated that they expected the government to tackle the media. This response was almost universal and came in the context of the question, what do they expect from the British government to make their school life better?

Effectively then, what the public understand about Muslims in general and British Muslims in particular is understood to deeply related to 'British Muslim representation' not only in the media but also in the whole social systems of the West. Representation is not only about perception, the position of the reader and audience is very critical. That is why non-British Muslims and British Muslims do not have a similar understanding of Muslim representation in the media (Hill, 1981, Fregoso, 1993 and Hall, 1997).

THE ROLE OF THE OCCIDENT IN ENGLISH LITERATURE

It is widely believed that the institutionalization of Europe's 'Other' began in the late eighteenth century and that it is directly linked to the rise of colonialism and imperialism in the nineteenth century. Nonetheless, Europe's knowledge of the Orient was developed through many centuries of discourse. Orientalists are the heirs to a long tradition of European writing, which was founded by people like Aeschylus and Homer. In *The Persians*, by Aeschylus for example, Asia is presented as a land of disaster, loss, and emptiness, and it seems that such literary texts as well as other writings in general played a pivotal role in the creation of 'the Other'.

After the rise of Christendom and subsequently Islam, Orientalism gained greater significance as the encounters between the two religions increased. Indeed, some scholars believe that the foundations of Orientalism were established by the Christian scholar John of Damascus, who was a close companion of the Ummayad Caliph Yazid. He claimed that Islam was a pagan cult and that the Holy *Ka'aba* was an idol. He also claimed among other things that the Prophet of Islam was utterly corrupt. (Sardar, 1999).

The wilful misunderstanding of Islam and the 'Orient' grew and intensified as Islam continued its rise. However, the Crusades provided the perfect opportunity for Christian scholars and politicians to create a monolithic and supposedly demonic Islam that stood opposed to Christendom; this allowed Europeans to believe that they had the right to subjugate and own the land where Christianity was born. The Crusades had an enormous and long-lasting impact on 'Western' society and as a result it became a major theme in Western thinking and literature. Works such as *The Song of Roland* (12th - 14th Century), *Songs of Geste* (12th -15th Century), *Don Sebastian* (Dryden, 1809), *Irene* (Johnson, 1749), *Rasselas* (Johnson, 1759) and many others are highly influenced by the ideas behind the Crusades and helped to further distort the image of Islam and Muslims through constructed misrepresentations and knowledgeable ignorance. The same can clearly be seen in major literary works such as *The Inferno* (Dante, 1306-1314), where the Prophet Mohammad and Ali bin Abi Talib are seen being horribly tortured in Dante's hell.

As a result of the Renaissance and the Reformation, when modern concepts of the West were being formulated, a new stance towards the 'Other' was produced. European thinkers claimed that as a result of the emergence of the rationalist scientific viewpoint, the West has moved beyond the Ancient 'Western' civilizations, let alone the achievements of Islamic, Indian, and Chinese civilizations. While the medieval attitudes towards the East were retained, the Orient was now transmuted from rich and powerful to poor, inferior, and incompetent.

In *Culture and Imperialism (1993)*, Said points out how the nineteenth-century novel played a critical role in the actual formation and enforcement of Empire. He also stresses the indispensable role that culture plays in the development of imperialism. Modern Europeans are shown to be justifying imperialism as they imagine themselves as being on a civilizing mission rather than on a mission of plunder. They view their own culture as "the best that has been thought and said" (Arnold, 1865, p. 15). Therefore, colonial discourse tends to exclude or minimize reference to European exploitation of 'the Other', while repeatedly pointing to the 'barbaric' nature of the subjugate peoples. This process often takes place without the individual colonizing subject even being consciously aware of it. This is what is often viewed as the Western method of domination.

Through this Eurocentric discourse of superior wisdom and moral neutrality, a relatively monolithic and homogeneous 'Other' encompassing most of the world east and south of Europe was created. The Orient, in other words, has actually been constructed by the neutralizing of the stereotypes and assumptions of Orientalists. However, what makes Said's *Orientalism* so relevant and significant today is arguably the way in which he maps the discriminatory strategies of this discourse both diachronically and synchronically right into the contemporary period, even though the centre of power has shifted from Europe to the United States.

Western assumptions of cultural superiority have roots so deep that even the social reform movements, such as the working class, the liberal, and the feminist movements were all more or less imperialistic. None of these movements ever seriously touched upon the assumptions of imperialist culture. In literary circles today, writers like Carlyle, Dickens, Eyre, Ruskin, and Thackeray, who believed in colonial expansion and showed obvious signs of racial prejudice in their works, are all viewed as people of culture whose works are an integral part of the Western cultural heritage. Their views on blacks and other 'peripheral' races are regarded as of lesser importance and forgivable in comparison to their enormous cultural contribution.

Said proposes a model of worldly criticism and he criticizes much of contemporary literary theory, due to its detachment from the problems existing in the real world. When he says that texts are worldly, he means "they are…a part of the social world, human life, and of course the historical moments in which they are located and interpreted" (Said, 1984, p. 4). Hence, if texts are worldly, then criticism must also deal with the world.

Said's commitment to worldly criticism can be seen more clearly in *Culture and Imperialism*, where he employs a mode of reading which he calls 'contrapuntal'. A contrapuntal reading is a way for "reading back" and providing counterpoints to the texts of Western literature, in order to reveal the extent to which they are implicated in the process of imperialism, colonialism, and neo-colonialism, so e.g. a contrapuntal reading of Joseph Conrad finds him complicit with the totalizing assumptions of colonialism despite being anti-imperialist (Said uses Conrad's *Heart of Darkness*, 1905). According to Said, Conrad's knowledge of Africans has no more to do with any personal experience he may have gained in his 1890 African adventure than with a long-lasting politicized and ideological tradition of Africanism (Said, 1994). While he is sceptical about imperial expansion, the portrayal of an almost evil primitiveness among black Africans along with the derogatory and dehumanizing representation of Africa and Africans actually serves to help justify the mission of imperialism.

A re-reading of the early 19th century canonical novel *Jane Eyre* by Charlotte Bronte in this light is for numerous reasons even more productive. In this work one can see feminist Orientalist discourse permeating the work. Charlotte Bronte displaces a western source of patriarchal oppression onto an Oriental society, which allows English readers to ponder local problems without having to question how they define themselves as Westerners and Christians. As is the case with many other Western proto-feminist writers such as Wollstonecraft, Anna Jameson, Elizabeth Gaskell, and Elizabeth Barrett Browning, by figuring objectionable aspects of life in the West as Eastern in essence, she in fact defines her ultimate objective as eliminating Eastern contamination from Western life. Jane Eyre views Rochester as a Western man who is under the corruptive influence of Eastern ideas. The shawls, the turban, his 'Persian' laws, and arrogance, as well as his 'Oriental-like' attitude towards women, must be dealt with in order for him to be redeemed and thoroughly westernized.

Contemporary feminists such as Sandra M. Gilbert and Susan Gubar simply perceive Jane Eyre as a proto-feminist heroine who achieves victory over an oppressive and patriarchal world. However, as Gayatri Chakravorty Spivak points out, Jane Eyre is implicated in colonialism on at least two levels (Spivak, 1985, p. 262-80). As in Mansfield Park, one must assume that her inheritance, which includes the wealth that she bestows upon her cousin, St. John Rivers the Christian missionary, comes from the slave trade. Hence, like Rochester her freedom and independence is founded upon the enslavement of numerous people who are of a different colour and race.

In addition, Jane's representations of the 'Other' illustrates that, like Rochester, she holds a fundamental belief in her own racial superiority.

Rochester's wife Bertha Mason, referred to by Jane as a "clothed hyena" (Bronte, 1991, p. 296), is a Creole with savage, lurid, and dark features. The idea that people born of parents from different races are more animal-like is an often-repeated assumption in colonial discourse. Added to this are the passages on the Orient, where women are all ignorant "Harem inmates", who need a western woman like Jane to "preach liberty to them" (Bronte, 1991, p. 272). To add to this there is Rochester's depiction of Jamaica as a hellish, maddening, and apocalyptic land:

> "[…] being unable to sleep in bed, I got up and opened the window. The air was like Sulphur-streams – I could find no refreshment anywhere. Mosquitoes came buzzing in and hummed sullenly round the room; the sea, which I could hear from thence, rumbled dull like an earthquake – black clouds were casting up over it; the moon was setting in the waves, broad and red, like a hot cannon-ball – she threw her last bloody glance over a world quivering with the ferment of tempest. I was physically influenced by the atmosphere and scene, and my ears were filled with the curses the maniac [Bertha] still shrieked out" (Bronte, 1991, p. 312)

However, his deliverance from potential madness or even suicide comes in the form of a fresh wind from Europe:

> "The sweet wind from Europe was still whispering in the refreshed leaves, and the Atlantic was thundering in glorious liberty; my heart, dried up and scorched for a long time, swelled to the stone, and filled with living blood – my being longed for renewal – my soul thirsted for a pure draught. I saw my hope revive – and felt regeneration possible. From a flowery arch at the bottom of my garden I gazed over the sea – bluer than the sky: the old world was beyond; clear prospects opened." (Bronte, 1991, p. 312-13)

By the end of the novel, like St. John who "labours for his race" (Bronte, 1991, p. 457) in India, Rochester becomes a true Christian, through relinquishing all of his former Eastern traits.

A contrapuntal reading of Lord Byron's Orientalist poems will reveal that his works also work within a similar discourse. Byron in this sense is more significant and interesting than most other writers of his age, as he actually travelled to and experienced the Orient. Therefore, it is important to gauge the extent to which Byron's Orientalist preconceptions are able to survive contact with reality as well as the extent to which they are modified. It is also important to understand the extent to which the correctness and truthfulness of his Oriental representations were deemed as important by the poet as well as how and why his writings on the Orient were and still are widely regarded as reliable among literary scholars and critics. The fact that even modern critics regularly take it for granted that his observations were and are still valid, shows that his emphasis on reliability, along with his representations, fit in well with the dominant stereotypes of more contemporary Orientalism.

In *The Bride of Abydos* the typical Eastern stereotypes are displayed, as Oriental men are divided into two categories. They are either despots or they are "brave" and "gallant" slaves who mindlessly await their "Lord's behest" (p. 1, 22). Giaffir's face is typically Muslim. "Not oft betrays to standers by/ the mind within, well skill'd to hide/ All but unconquerable pride" (p. 1, 27-9). Muslims hide their true thoughts from others, a feature which makes them unknowable, mysterious, and untrustworthy. Of course, this does not include Byron, who can see through this mask, as the English traveller knows more about 'Orientals' than the 'Orientals' themselves. According to Byron, all Muslims are despots who even treat their own sons as slaves. The "son of Moslem must expire,/ Ere dare to sit before his sire" (1, 51-52) and, according to the 'authentic' Muslim Giaffir, "We Moslem reck not much of blood" (p. 1, 200).

Readers of contemporary fiction confront an almost identical discourse on the Orient, thus reinforcing the belief that a monolithic East which is both timeless and barbaric actually exists. Evil and barbaric Muslims are determined to destroy the United States as the standard-bearer of freedom and democracy. This can be seen clearly in works such as John Updike's *The Coup*, John Randall's *The Jihad Ultimatum*, Phillip Caputo's *Horn of Africa*, as well as Frederick Forsyth's *The Fist of God*. The open racism in these works is quite shocking, as the white, civilized, polite, and humane characters are almost the complete opposite of the filthy brown and bloodthirsty Muslim antagonists.

Muslims are also generally depicted as inferior, incompetent, and incapable of ruling themselves. In Michael Carson's *Friends and Infidels* as well as James Clavell's *Escape*, such characteristics are obvious and the racism is more than skin deep. In *Escape*, regardless of the fact that the author has no understanding of Iran, let alone the events surrounding the Islamic Revolution, he demonstrates Oriental inferiority through admissions made by Iranian characters. The Khan admits to Erikka that "We are an Oriental people, not Western, who understand violence and torture" (Clavell, 1996, p. 72). Another similarity between this construction and that presented by Byron, almost two centuries ago, is where the reader is told that almost all Iranians wear masks "All the kindness, politeness" is "only on the surface" (Clavell, 1996, p. 52). Iranians are portrayed as filthy (Clavell, p. 91), irrational, and incapable of comprehending the mind of a Westerner (Clavell, p. 80). Iranian women do not believe that they are or ever can be equal to men (Clavell, p. 152). Religious men who come face to face with women wearing Western clothes on the streets, harass them, shout insults, expose themselves (Clavell, p. 158).

It seems obvious that a certain discursive regularity exists or persists in the ethnocentric processes of Orientalist writers of the nineteenth century and contemporary writers. While the relationship between East and West can assume highly dissimilar manifestations, the Westerner rarely loses the upper hand. This flexible positional superiority bolsters the assertion that Orientalism is an ideologically loaded discourse with severely bounded borders.

Another significant trend in recent decades within Orientalist discourse is the indigenous Orientalism that can be seen in the works of certain scholars and thinkers. These writers are sometimes referred to as 'captive minds', 'brown sahibs', or 'native informants', a concept which is somewhat similar to what Malcolm X would call the 'house Negro' (Rudnick, Smith, and Rubin, 2006, p. 123). These local Orientalists are defined by their intellectual bondage with and dependence on the West. A captive mind is not uncritical; it is for the most part critical on behalf of the West. According to one critic, the 'Orientalized Oriental' is:

> "[…] one who physically resides in the 'East', and sometimes in the West, yet spiritually feeds on the West. S/he announces her/himself to be 'post-Oriental', or 'postcolonial', yet is a practicing member of the 'orientalising' praxis in its daily operations in the interpenetrating realms of art, aesthetics, folklore, media, education, and so on. S/he is the non-Western subject who makes her/himself largely in the image of the West, its experiences, designs, and its expectations…for her/him the West is always more intelligible and fulfilling, and thus more attractive than the East". (Soguk, 1993, p. 363)

According to Sardar, "V.S. Naipaul and Salman Rushdie are undoubtably the most notorious brown sahibs of recent times" (Sardar, 1999, p. 88). Such writers persistently attempt to support 'progressive' Western secular culture against the 'menacing darkness' of Islam, through language that has been traditionally used by Orientalists depicting Orientals as homogeneous, inferior, irrational, savage, despotic, fatalistic, and Oriental women as sensual and submissive. In Naipaul's *Among the Believers: an Islamic Journey*, published in the early 1980s where he writes about his travels through Iran, Pakistan, Malaysia, and Indonesia, although he admits his ignorance about Islam, he is able to judge it as monolithic and inferior.

> "The glories of this religion were in the remote past; it has generated nothing like a Renaissance. Muslim countries, where not colonies, were despotisms; and nearly all, before oil, were poor". (Naipaul, 2001, 13)

He also sees it as a timeless land, unlike the West which is dynamic by nature. He begins the chapter with a paragraph from James Morier's *The Adventures of Hajji Baba of Ispahan* (1824), a well known Orientalist text that depicts Iran in a very negative light. However, what is important is that Naipaul seems to imply that there is little difference between the Iran of the 1980's and that of the early nineteenth century. Like the rest of the monolithic Orient, it is backward, static, and in almost every way inferior.

Naipaul also generalizes in a similar fashion about Iran and Iranians. When he meets Sadeq, who was to go with him to the holy city of Qom, he says "He was the kind of man who, without political doctrine, only with resentments, had made the Iranian revolution" (Naipaul, 2001, p. 3). He later adds that "there was a lot of the Iranian hysteria and confusion locked up in his smiling eyes" (Naipaul, 2001, p. 5). He is able to stereotype Iranians even though he admits his ignorance about Iran, Iranian history, and the revolution. (Naipaul, 2001). Indeed, one can see the extent of his supposed 'knowledge' through the many quotes he uses that supposedly belong to *Ayatollah* Khomeini. Most of them are either distorted or just cannot be found in any reliable text.

The same language of authority is repeatedly used to describe the other three countries and their peoples. Apparently, the sophisticated Western or Westernized man does not need to know a great deal about a Muslim country, its language, culture, or people to be able to judge it, as the people are mentally inferior, monolithic, and ignorant. Pakistanis (especially those who are religious), for example, are described as utterly ignorant and inferior like the teacher at the theological school (Naipaul, 2001, p. 105). Indeed, they readily admit that they are a "bad" nation (Naipaul, 2001; 104).

Similar discursive practices can be easily seen in Salman Rushdie's *The Satanic Verses*, where the author parodies and ridicules Islam with sheer arrogance. According to Sardar:

> *The Satanic Verses* is [...] an exercise in undermining both the sacred history of Islam and the very personality that defines Muslims as Muslims and thus to erase the entire cultural and religious identity of Muslim people. Such an exercise could not be attempted without recycling the potent images of Orientalism; Rushdie relies on these images to such an extent that his fictionalized Muhammad is dubbed Mahound, the Devil's synonym from *chansons de geste* (Sardar, 1991, p. 91)!

To the Westernized Oriental, civilization means the West and cultures are positioned in a hierarchical order with Western civilization placed at the centre.

Another example of colonial surrogacy can be found in works such as those of Azar Nafisi, which confirm what Orientalist representations had always claimed, the backwardness and inferiority of Muslims and Islam. Along with many fashionable 'memoirs' of Muslim women Nafisi's *Reading Lolita in Tehran*, confirms stereotypes about Islam and Muslims that maker her memoir an ideological icon rather than a personal account of life in Iran. Nafisi, whose family was among the elite during the Pahlavi dynasty, displays an extraordinary amount of contempt towards anything that has to do with Islam. Religious men like Nasrin's uncle are rapists (Nafisi, 2004, p. 48) and "perverts" (Nafisi, 2004, p. 210), and their female counterparts are no better (Nafisi, 2004, p. 168 and p. 211). Indeed, such sexual perversion can be seen in their religious rites as well as in their ideology. In their religious ceremonies, one could feel "a wild, sexually flavored frenzy in the air" (Nafisi, 2004, 90) and when the millions of Iranians who took part in the funeral ceremony of *Ayatollah* Khomeini were sprayed at intervals with water to cool them off because of the extreme heat Nafisi claims that "the effect made the scene oddly sexual" (p. 244). However, it is not just all the religious men and women in Iran who are perverts, but Iranian men who live in the United States are almost as bad. It seems they too, like almost everyone else, are obsessed with Nafisi.

> "I shunned the company of the Iranian community, especially the men, who had numerous illusions about a young divorcee's availability" (p. 83).

The lines above seem to give new meaning to Nafisi's claim that "our culture shunned sex because it was too involved with it" (p. 304). Nevertheless, this discourse of demonisation has implications that go beyond the 'East'. Those minority cultures and ethnic groups residing in the 'West' are affected by such constructions.

As stated, the ideology of religious and pious Muslim men is even worse. In this regard Nafisi makes some of her wildest accusations. Nafisi tells a story that she claims to have heard from what appears to be a former member of the anti-Iranian government terrorist organisation MKO, based in Saddam's Iraq, about a girl held in an Iranian prison.

> "There was one girl there – her only sin had been her amazing beauty. They brought her in on some trumped-up immorality charge. They kept her for over a month and repeatedly raped her. They pass her from one guard to another. The story got around jail very fast, because the girl wasn't even political; she wasn't with the political prisoners. They married the virgins off to the guards, who would later execute them. The philosophy behind this act was that if they were killed as virgins, they would go to heaven." (Nafisi, 2004, p. 212)

What makes these accusations especially significant and dangerous is that she associates them with Islam and the ideology of those whom she opposes. As with Naipaul, she frequently 'quotes' *Ayatollah* Khomeini, despite no records of any such quotes. It is a pervading critique of work that deals with post-revolutionary Iran that any manner of outrageous and often offensive statement can be attributed to *Ayatollah* Khomeini without it actually existing. So demonic is the portrayal of *Ayatollah* Khomeini that any manner of vicious statement can be unquestionably attributed to him. Most quotes are inaccurate, misleading, or nonexistent. This is a rather curious point, as Nafisi's account suggests that she has almost total recall, even though she admits paradoxically that she does not have a very precise memory (Nafisi, 2004, p. 161).

Nafisi also seems to have lived in a very secluded world while in Iran, as she seems to know little about people and events other than those she sees or hears about in her small circle. She implies that Iran was responsible for the first Gulf war rather than Saddam Hussein; she makes the ludicrous claim that 10-16 year-old Iranian military combatants carried out "human wave" attacks (Nafisi, 2004, p. 208) and were "promised of keys to a heaven where they could finally enjoy all the pleasures from which they had abstained in life" (Nafisi, 2004, p. 209). Elsewhere, she says that at her university there were two legally recognized student organizations one of which was called "Islamic Jihad" (Nafisi, 2004, p. 193). However, there has never been such an organization active in any Iranian university. She also attacks and ridicules the Iranian cinema of the 1980s calling it "propaganda" (Nafisi, 2004, p. 206), even though Iranian cinema actually became internationally famous and acclaimed during that decade.

Nafisi sees salvation for Iranians as possible only through English literature, Western values, a Western education (Nafisi, 2004, 281) or even a green card (Nafisi, 2004, p. 285). When the favourite uncle of Yassi, a disciple of Nafisi's, who lives in the United States, comes to Iran for a vacation, he puts new ideas into her head. He is unlike anyone else in the family and has a very positive influence on Yassi. His exceptional personality and moral influence is clearly linked to the fact that he lives in the United States. In the words of Nafisi:

> "Now he advised her to continue her studies in America. Everything he told Yassi about life in America – events that seemed routine to him – gained a magical glow in her greedy eyes." (Nafisi, 2004, p. 270)

Among the many people who she has unjustly caricatured in her book were university lecturers (Nafisi, 2004, p. 294-4) and professors (Nafisi, 2004, p. 69 and p. 99), who are left without voices, except for the ones she has imposed upon them. Nafisi is, of course, the hero in this tale, as she taught Nabakov to her eight disciples secretly in Tehran "against all odds" (p. 6). She forgets to mention, however, that at the time, her rival the hated Professor X among others had students at the University of Tehran who wrote their theses on Nabakov.

The ideologisation of her work beyond personal biography is exemplified by her desire to speak authoritatively on behalf of all Iranians and claims that "We" Iranians "living in the Islamic Republic of Iran grasped both the tragedy and absurdity of the cruelty to which we were subjected" (Nafisi, 2004, p. 23) by the government. However, she contradicts herself elsewhere and states that there were many young students on campus who were 'fanatical' (Nafisi, 2004, p. 250-1). She clearly understands the mentality of all those whom she opposes, because they are inferior, simple-minded, and crude. She represents herself as the superior, Westernized intellectual authority, who can grasp all these things and even more. After the demise of *Ayatollah* Khomeini millions of people in Tehran took part in the funeral procession. Hence, one can assume that all these people were among the worthless and uneducated fanatics who stand beneath Nafisi, the intellectual.

Marjane Satrapi's *Persepolis: the Story of a Childhood* is in many ways almost identical to Nafisi's *Reading Lolita in Tehran*. Iranians are portrayed as both dishonest and foolish (Satrapi, 2003, p. 32) and Satrapi's explanations regarding Muslim beliefs and culture (Satrapi, 2003, p. 94-6) are unfounded and misleading. Here, too, the fantastic story about the key to heaven is repeated. According to the family maid, her son was given a plastic key painted in gold at school:

"They gave this to my son at school. They told the boys that if they went to war and were lucky enough to die, this key would get them into heaven […] All my life I've been faithful to the religion. If it's come to this […] Well I can't believe in anything anymore". (Satrapi, 2003, p. 99)

Like Nafisi, she makes the extraordinary claim that children are taken to the war fronts, hypnotized, and thrown into battle to be slaughtered (Satrapi, 2003, p, 101). History is further distorted to make it appear that the Islamic Republic was to blame for the war and had actually "admitted that the survival of the regime depended on the war" (Satrapi, 2003, p. 114-16). Also there is the repetition of the accusation that girls are taken to jail, forced to marry their jailors, effectively raped, and then executed (Satrapi, p. 145). Both texts work within a single Western Orientalist discourse of demonisation, hostile to Muslims and Islam.

Oddly, in *Reading Lolita in Tehran* there is a reference to another memoir, Betty Mahmoody's *Not Without my Daughter* (Nafisi, 2004, p. 324). In this work Mahmoody, who briefly lived in Iran, tells her version of life in the country and her escape from the country and her husband. In this story she speaks about the irresolvable differences between Eastern and Western cultures. Iranians are filthy (pp15, 23, 27, 28, 31, 32, 36, 37, 85, 231, 335, 365), scheming (p. 220), corrupt (p. 17), violent (p. 21), hostile (p. 342), lazy (p. 429), eager to kill (p. 203), unorganized (p. 35), unpredictable (p. 342) and animal-like:

"Sitting on the floor cross-legged or perched on one knee, the Iranians attacked the meal like a herd of untamed animals desperate for food. The only utensils provided were large ladle-like spoons. Some used these in tandem with their hands or a portion of bread folded into a scoop; others did not bother with spoons. Within seconds there was food everywhere. It was shoveled indiscriminately into chattering mouths that spilled and dribbled bits and pieces […]. The unappetizing scene was accompanied by a cacophony of Farsi". (Mahmoody, p. 26)

In this "strange society" (p. 45) large numbers of children suffer from "birth defects or deformities of one kind or another. Others had a peculiar, vacant expression" (p. 28). Daily showering is viewed as a strange American custom (p. 42) to the "hordes" of "grim-faced" Iranians (p. 43). The country is a "strange symphony of the damned" full of beggars who go from door to door crying for help and struggling for survival" (p. 114).

According to Mahmoody, some Iranians attempt to copy western culture, but fail due to their lack of sophistication. This literally meant that she did not like the taste of Iranian Pizzas (p. 116). Iranians also pay homage to anyone who has been educated in the United States.

Her construction of the Iranian psyche is extraordinary. They are childlike, inferior, ignorant, and do not seem to know what is good for them. Hence, within such an Orientalist framework it is understandable for her to claim that "Time seems to mean nothing to the average Iranian" (p. 81) or that "Once a year everyone in Iran takes a bath".(p. 207).

An Iranian, of course, would probably counter that she knew nothing about Iranians or their customs, or that, assuming that she is honest, she is so prejudiced that she cannot comprehend anything that contradicts her claims. Mahmoody herself states that she "did not care a thing about Iranian customs" (p. 84). Her extraordinary comments about Iranian men, her utter ignorance about Islamic history (p. 89), Islam (p. 91, 309), Islamic law (p.170), or Iranian laws (p. 288), reflect the fact that her 'knowledge' is derived from western sources rather than from real experiences in this "horrid land" (p.132). Hence, like Nafisi and Satrapi, she too could claim that:

> "Whenever the *pasdar* arrested a woman who was to be executed, the men raped her first, because they had a saying: 'A woman should never die a virgin'"(Mahmoody, p. 366).

Significantly, the reasons why girls are supposedly raped in prison differ completely, according to these three authors. However, when the Orient is being discussed such obvious contradictions do not affect the story's credibility. Such actions are to be expected in such a "mad country" (Mahmoody, p. 391).

Perhaps one of the most extraordinary claims made in the novel is where the writer claims that in Iran women are not allowed to show their faces (Mahmoody, p. 367). Indeed the picture on the cover of the Corgi edition published in 1989 shows a woman whose face, except for her eyes, is completely covered by a veil. However, the fact is that in Iran women do not use veils and they do not cover their faces.

Such representations are not limited to Iran. Jean Sasson's trilogy *Princess, Daughters of Arabia*, and *Desert Royal* depicts Arab Muslims in a similar light. The trilogy is about the life of 'Sultana' who is supposedly a Saudi Arabian princess and closely related to the King. Saudi Arabia is a closed society with an authoritarian ruler and a royal family that has control over large amounts of the country's oil wealth, with the backing of western countries, and 'Sultana' is a woman who lives a secluded life. Nevertheless, she stereotypes people of the country (Sasson, 1993, p. 226). In *Princess*, Sultana states that "women in my land are ignored by their fathers, scorned by their brothers, and abused by their husbands (Sasson, 1993, p. 22). While it is true that the official government ideology and policy is oppressive to women, it is by no means a fact that all men and women of that country all have similar characteristics. Indeed, if there is oppression and injustice, Sultana plays a part in it as she is a senior member and supporter of the ruling family who justifies and benefits from their oppressive rule (Sasson, 1993, p. 248).

In the same book, Sasson goes even further and stereotypes all Arabs, which presumably includes all people from Morocco to Iraq (Sasson, 1993, p. 60, 275), even though most of the people she knows are from the royal family. In contrast, Americans and Westerners in general are presented as friendly, patient (Sasson, 1993, p. 62-3, 81, 258), and saviours (Sasson, 1993, p. 283). A western education is a necessity for anyone to be able to have progressive ideas (Sasson, 1993, p.148) and even contact with a Westerner can spare people from barbaric customs (Sasson, 1993, p. 159) as they are bearers of knowledge (Sasson, 1993, p.161). The same discourse can be seen in *Daughters of Arabia* and *Desert Royal* as well as in works such as Hanan al-Shaykh's *Women of Sand and Myrrh*.

The translation of many of these stereotypes into modern popular fiction is perhaps best exemplified by the Bridget Jones' books (*Bridget Jones' Diary*, 1997 and *Bridget Jones: The Edge of Reason*, 2001) and columns in *The Independent* newspaper. Both books have been turned into films, and the Bridget Jones phenomenon has been important in creating a whole new genre of literature with mass popularity aimed at women i.e. 'chick lit'.

Despite being a flippant, and highly comical look at the life, loves (and lack thereof) and woes of the eponymous heroine and the women she is clearly meant to symbolise, the Bridget Jones' novels and columns invoke the Oriental other that repeatedly make Bridget's often pitiful existence, social faux pas and disastrous love life seem exemplary. Whilst the first novel – a reworking of author Helen Fielding's popular newspaper columns, carries largely racial representations of otherness, the sequel employs Islamophobia. In the first novel, Bridget's ignorance of other races is often used as device to both deprecate and endear the reader to the heroine. Thus Bridget's inability to understand the significant difference between Norway and Pakistan and the fact that sparkling wine she just bought cheaply and cannot remember the origin of is hardly likely to have come from Pakistan (or for that matter Norway) is a point for sympathy rather than consternation on the part of the reader – Bridget is after all depressed over her weight and lack of love life (p. 18).

Her (and her supposedly intellectual, Cambridge educated) boyfriend's inability to understand the difference between Bosnians and Serbs and identify which might be Muslim (p. 157 – 8) is a point of comic relief and their discussion during a wedding ceremony on what happened in Srebrenica (the site of the worst massacre on European soil since WWII) is punctuated with references about the 'bride's tits'. Having been dumped later in the book by said boyfriend, Bridget's friend Tom consoles her with the trivialising words, 'Bloody git, Daniel. If that man turns out to be single handedly responsible for all the fighting in Bosnia, I wouldn't be in the least surprised.'(p. 190)

Genocide of Muslims in the Bridget Jones context is about as serious as being dumped by the charming yet caddish, Daniel Cleaver. In the second novel, the trauma of the Bosnian Muslim experience is again lampooned, when Bridget overhears her friend telling off her young children when she telephones hers:

> "There was a loud crashing noise followed by the sound of running water and screaming in manner of Muslims being massacred by Serbs with 'Mummy will smack! She will smack!' as if on a loop in the background. "(p. 11)

At the end of the first novel however, comes the ideological crunch. On lamenting over another lonely and miserable Christmas, the heroine writes in her diary:

> '…I hate Christmas. Everything is designed for families, romance, warmth, emotion and presents, and if you have no boyfriend, no money, your mother is going out with a missing Portuguese criminal, and your friends don't want to be your friends any more, it makes you want to emigrate to a vicious Muslim regime, where at least all the women are treated like social outcasts.' (p. 290)

Both Bridget Jones' novels convey the idea of sensuous, oversexed and lascivious Eastern / Muslim men. Her mother's lover is derided as a 'Omar Sharif-figure with a gentleman's handbag' (p. 56) and the second novel begins Bridget describing her happiness as:

> "… marvellous, [fell] rather like Jemima Goldsmith or similar radiant newlywed opening cancer hospital in veil while everyone imagines her in bed with Imran Khan." (p. 3)

Later in the same novel, her friend recounts a tale of a friend, saying:

> "'I knew someone who slept with a Turk once,' said Jude. 'And he had a penis so enormous he couldn't sleep with anyone'" (p. 99)

Sex, Islam and the Muslim male as a pejorative image recurs again with religious text being reduced to the level of a satirised self-help sex book on more than one occasion:

> "'And you just know every move you make is being dissected by committee of girlfriends according to some breathtakingly arbitrary code made up of *Buddhism Today, Venus and Buddha Have a Shag* and the Quran." (p. 253)

Further 'If Mohammed Dated' (p. 264) is considered a possible title to another ridiculous self-help book. As the hero of both novels, Mark Darcy states with authority (he unlike Daniel Cleaver is aware of racial and religious differences), not only are self-help books he sees on Bridget's shelf the stuff of nonsense, Islam in particular has nothing to give in this fad which often borrows from Eastern cultures, stating:

> "'So what's that then? Not a Muslim, I hope. I don't think you find much forgiveness in a faith that lops people's hands for stealing bread buns.'" (p. 76)

Whilst the Bridget Jones' books do not deal with Muslim or Islamic themes, the pejorative referencing of Islam and Muslims illustrates again unquestioning stereotypes and generalisations from which the Western heroine can build her identity – however abysmal and laughable at various points that identity is.

In a recent return to the pages of The Independent, Bridget Jones, now back with Daniel Cleaver (2006) is rushed to hospital to give birth to their baby. This time, and within the smaller surrounds of a newspaper column, the association of Islam and Muslims with barbarity, lack of civilisation and education is profound and demeaning and constitutes a right wing narrative against immigrants, minorities and asylum seekers. Daniel Cleaver, whilst arguing with Bridget about the decrepit state of the NHS hospital they are in states:

> "I've never seen so many pregnant Muslims in my life. You'll end up getting a clitoridectomy. Half the signs are in bloody Arabic."

In one paragraph, the author has confused concerns over the standards of an NHS hospital, the fears of cultural takeover and the idea of female genital mutilation all somehow linked to (pregnant) Muslims.

BEYOND OCCIDENT / ORIENT

The purpose of these analyses is not to invert the discursive process, reclaiming an objective East so that it can be held up as the superior of the Western 'Other'; it is about the moral status of the different cultures and ideologies of the people of the Orient. The concept that an Orient and Occident actually exist and divide humanity into two distinct oceans seems to be a fictitious ideological construction, which is in some ways relatively homogeneous. It is not the purpose of this chapter either to posit a single, objective West which constructs the 'Other', given that constructions of 'the Other' are in certain significant ways not notably heterogeneous. One must add, however, that to a large extent visions of the East in English literature present the East as diverse in character and structure.

'Objectivity' itself becomes a device for power, both in the discourse and in the individual/system that produced the discourse. One who works within this severely bounded area of social knowledge assumes that the line separating 'us' from 'them' is objectively drawn. The views of 'the Other' are intolerant and derisory and it is assumed that there is no need to sustain this position with confirmation from local scholarship; it is deemed self-evident.

Such discursive strategies are not simply autonomous or independent acts of cultural production. They occur within particular political and social contexts and, in turn, they reinforce and sometimes help shape those contexts. Such discursive processes can often be found in the works of Western writers, as well as in the works of what Appiah calls the "comprador intelligentsia", as has been seen (Appiah, 1991, p. 348). It would have been surprising for the researcher to conclude otherwise, as the material in this chapter fits in well with patterns existing within the more global and explicitly political Orientalist discourse. Policy making and media circles in many Western countries regularly demonstrate belligerent hostility and manufacture exaggerated stereotypes, which even critics of Orientalism such as Said and Chomsky, often fail to recognize.

This dominant strategy of discourse and power does not merely produce 'West' or 'East', rather 'the Other' becomes the millions of people whose lives are reduced to caricatures and prejudices through this approach. While there are certainly issues of class, ethnicity, and gender within the East just as in the West, these issues are distorted by literary and non-literary presentations in both the past and present. These people are not only those living east or south of Europe; rather they are also the tens of millions of Muslims who are citizens of Western European and North American countries. Through this hegemonic discourse, even these citizens of Western societies, though not physically coerced into believing or living out dominant ideas or ideologies, are often psychologically forced to concede to them. Hegemonic consent to these ideas comes about as a result of their becoming so naturalized that such ideas are viewed as 'common sense'. Hence, while within Western societies many may view these citizens with suspicion and often contempt, what is even worse is that as a result of this powerful discourse some members of these religious, racial, and cultural minority groups may even come to see themselves as inferior and barbaric.

PART TWO: CONTEXTUAL ANALYSIS - BRITISH MUSLIM UNDERSTANDING OF MUSLIM REPRESENTATION IN THE MEDIA

This part deals with the analyses of qualitative and quantitative data. The tables that are included in this part firstly give information about the respondents i.e. geographical location, age group and gender etc. followed by tables in which the view of respondents regarding the representation of Muslims in the media. At this level quantitative data offers great assistance in terms of acquiring the precise views and feelings of the respondents, regarding their positioning and views on media discourse.

GEOGRAPHICAL LOCATION AND PERCEPTION OF MEDIA

According to table 5, respondents from Manchester (73.0%) and Peterborough (70.4%) are the most concerned about the Islamophobic portrayal of Muslims. London (65.5%) and Bradford (62.1%) closely followed these two cities in their concerns. The rates increased by addition of "racist" and "overtly fair representation but covertly destructive" rankings of the respondents. In this regard,

Luton (54.5%) and Swansea (50.0%) felt the media showed 'racism' rather than Islamophobia. In comparison to the ratings of other cities these figures are significantly large. However this might be explained by psychological theory that argues the surrounding circumstances influence the perception of people. Muslims may be isolated in such places or they may have a high concentration of a particular ethnic group in a particular area where there has been inter-ethnic tension with the local population. Therefore, they are very much vulnerable to racism and racial discrimination. In fact, the second volume of this project verifies that Muslims from Luton (91%) with a large Muslim minority reported the highest rate of discrimination in the UK (Ameli et al 2004b). Hence, racist attitudes in wider society might cause Muslims who live in these areas to perceive the Islamophobic stance of the media as racist.

Table 5: Location and Perception of Media

	I have no idea	Islamophobic	Racist	Fair representation of Muslims	Overtly fair representation but covertly destructive	TOTAL
Swansea	0 / .0%	5 / 31.3%	8 / 50.0%	1 / 6.3%	2 / 12.5%	16 / 100%
London	54 / 10.2%	347 / 65.5%	65 / 12.3%	21 / 4.0%	43 / 81.1%	530 / 100%
Birmingham	8 / 13.3%	33 / 55.0%	10 / 16.7%	2 / 3.3%	7 / 11.7%	60 / 100%
Manchester	0 / .0%	27 / 73.0%	5 / 13.5%	1 / 2.7%	4 / 10.8%	37 / 100%
Bradford	3 / 5.2%	36 / 62.1%	13 / 22.4%	2 / 3.4%	4 / 6.9%	58 / 100%
Glasgow	2 / 6.3%	16 / 50.0%	9 / 28.1%	1 / 3.1%	4 / 12.5%	32 / 100%
Newcastle	3 / 12.0%	12 / 48.0%	6 / 24.0%	1 / 4.0%	3 / 12.0%	25 / 100%
Cardiff	2 / 11.1%	10 / 55.6%	4 / 22.2%	1 / 5.6%	1 / 5.6%	18 / 100%
Oldham	3 / 21.4%	8 / 57.1%	2 / 14.3%	0 / .0%	1 / 7.1%	14 / 100%
Other	10 / 4.6%	148 / 68.2%	31 / 14.3%	9 / 4.1%	19 / 8.8%	217 / 100%
Coventry	2 / 18.2%	4 / 36.4%	3 / 27.3%	1 / 9.1%	1 / 9.1%	11 / 100%
Gloucester	4 / 9.8%	20 / 48.8%	8 / 19.5%	3 / 7.3%	6 / 14.6%	41 / 100%
Slough	0 / .0%	15 / 53.6%	2 / 7.1%	0 / .0%	11 / 39.3%	28 / 100%
Peterborough	2 / 7.4%	19 / 70.4%	3 / 11.1%	1 / 3.7%	2 / 7.4%	27 / 100%
Luton	0 / .0%	2 / 18.2%	6 / 54.5%	1 / 9.1%	2 / 18.2%	11 / 100%
Total	93 / 8.3%	702 / 62.4%	175 / 15.6%	45 / 4.0%	110 / 9.8%	1125 / 100.0%

AGE GROUPS AND PERCEPTION OF MEDIA

According to Table 6 there is no significant difference between different age groups and their perceptions of the media. The 25-29 (71.6%) and 35-39 (71.1%) age groups almost returned the same figures in terms of perceiving the media as being Islamophobic and held the highest negative views respectively. On the other hand, the 15-19 age group stands out for finding the media the least Islamophobic (42.7%) among all age groups. However, this does not mean that they found media representation positive. Instead their response concentrated on racism, with respondents in this age group having the highest figure (25.9%) for considering the media racist. Muslim youths in this age bracket also considered the media as overtly fair but covertly destructive (10.8%).

Table 6:	Age Group and perception of Media						
	Age	I have no idea	Islamophobic	Racist	Fair representation of Muslims	Overtly fair representation but covertly destructive	TOTAL
	15-19	27 14.6%	79 42.7%	48 25.9%	11 5.9%	20 10.8%	185 100.0%
	20-24	14 5.2%	182 67.9%	37 13.8%	2 .7%	33 12.3%	268 100.0%
	25-29	8 4.1%	139 71.6%	17 8.8%	12 6.2%	18 9.3%	194 100.0%
	30-34	10 7.2%	95 68.3%	23 16.5%	1 .7%	10 7.2%	139 100.0%
	35-39	4 4.8%	59 71.1%	9 10.8%	3 3.6%	8 9.6%	83 100.0%
	40-45	5 6.3%	48 60.0%	15 18.8%	3 3.8%	9 11.3%	80 100.0%
	45-49	2 4.3%	33 70.2%	9 19.1%	0 .0%	3 6.4%	47 100.0%
	50 and above	23 17.8%	67 51.9%	17 13.2%	13 10.1%	9 7.0%	129 100.0%
	Total	93 8.3%	702 62.4%	45 15.6%	45 4.0%	110 9.8%	1125 100.0%

GENDER AND PERCEPTION OF MEDIA

In terms of gender, the figures suggest that males and females held similar feelings about media portrayal of Muslims. However, female respondents (63.3%) slightly exceeded the male respondents (61.9%) in their consideration of the media as Islamophobic and covertly destructive (female 11.7% and male 8.7%). It should be mentioned here that practising Muslim women have greatly suffered from media stereotyping as volume four in this series has shown (Ameli and Merali, 2006a). In volume two of this project (Ameli *et al*, 2004b), a study of the well-known case of Shabina Begum, clearly elaborated how the media demonised a 15-year-old girl who wanted to wear a *jilbaab* to school. After a process of searching the national papers from 16 June to 25 November 2004 the study found that there were 48 news pieces, columns and articles that covered Shabina's case. The analysis found that "in most comments she and her hijab have been synonymous with stupidity, irrationality, intolerance, evil, and lack of culture. "Most commentators from celebrities to ordinary readers, and even some Muslims hailed the courts decision in not allowing her to wear *jilbaab* and vilified her claim as unreasonable and evil" (Ameli et al 2004b, p51).

Table 7:	Gender and perception of Media					
Gender	I have no idea	Islamophobic	Racist	Fair representation of Muslims	Overtly fair representation but covertly destructive	TOTAL
Female	32 8.0%	254 63.3%	55 13.7%	13 3.2%	47 11.7%	401 100.0%
Male	61 8.4%	448 61.9%	120 16.6%	32 4.4%	63 8.7%	724 100.0%
Total	93 8.3%	702 62.4%	175 15.6%	45 4.0%	110 9.8%	1125 100.0%

BIRTHPLACE AND PERCEPTION OF MEDIA

Table 8 - place of birth and perception of media - contains a striking correlation. Those who were born in the UK held more pessimistic views regarding the media than those who were born abroad and migrated to the UK. This is counterintuitive in that it is usually presumed that those born outside the UK, probably in Muslim majority countries would have the opportunity to compare the media representation of Muslims in their own countries and find the British media more negative and biased. There might be two reasons for the findings: first, those who migrated from Muslim countries were ruled by aggressive secular regimes and experienced much more bias and negative Muslim portrayal in their media. Secondly, unlike those who have immigrated to the UK, those who are born in Britain interact and participate more in British society, and consequently, it is easier for them to detect any Islamophobic and racist portrayal in the media or elsewhere.

In support of the abovementioned argument the first volume of this project points to similar findings. That study found that the dissatisfaction with British society among British citizens is much higher than those of non-British Muslims. The table does not indicate whether the citizens were born in the UK. However, since they are British citizens, it is reasonable to assume that many, if not most, must have been resident for a considerable period in the UK.

Table 8: Place of Birth and perception of Media

Place of Birth	I have no idea	Islamophobic	Racist	Fair representation of Muslims	Overtly fair representation but covertly destructive	TOTAL
Britain	47 7.6%	388 63.1%	105 17.1%	15 2.4%	60 9.8%	615 100.0%
Other Countries	46 9.0%	314 61.6%	70 13.7%	30 5.9%	50 9.8%	510 100.0%
Total	93 8.3%	702 62.4%	175 15.6%	45 4.0%	110 9.8%	1125 100.0%

In addition, British Muslim citizens (63.4% Islamophobic, 15.5% racist and 9.4% covertly destructive) are more pessimistic than non-British Muslim citizens (9.9% Islamophobic, 15.7% racist and 13.2% overtly destructive) in their assessments of media portrayal.

Table 9: Citizenship Status and perception of Media

Citizenship	I have no idea	Islamophobic	Racist	Fair representation of Muslims	Overtly fair representation but covertly destructive	TOTAL
Yes	81 8.1%	637 63.4%	156 15.5%	36 3.6%	94 9.4%	1004 100.0%
No	12 9.9%	65 53.7%	19 15.7%	9 7.4%	16 13.2%	121 100.0%
Total	93 8.3%	702 62.4%	175 15.6%	45 4.0%	110 9.8%	1125 100.0%

These findings and especially figures in table 9 might suggest that intensive Islamophobic and racist attitudes in the media could be one of the major causes for the alienation of British Muslims from society. As table 10 verifies there is a correlation between negative perception of media and disaffiliation of Muslims to British society:

Table 10:	Affiliation and Perception of media					
	I have no idea	Islamophobic	Racist	Fair representation of Muslims	Overtly fair representation but covertly destructive	TOTAL
Yes, very strong	9 6.7%	78 57.8%	22 16.3%	13 9.6%	13 9.68%	135 100.0%
Yes, I feel a sense of belonging	19 5.9%	213 65.9%	45 13.9%	9 2.8%	37 11.5%	323 100.0%
Neutral	28 9.8%	162 56.6%	55 19.2%	12 4.2%	29 10.1%	286 100.0%
No, not at all	9 5.5%	124 75.2%	20 12.1%	3 1.8%	9 5.5%	165 100.0%
No, I don't feel a sense of belonging	4 2.7%	105 71.9%	20 13.7%	2 1.4%	15 10.3%	146 100.0%
I don't know	24 34.3%	20 28.6%	13 18.6%	6 8.6%	7 10.0%	70 100.0%
Total	93 8.3%	702 62.4%	175 15.6%	45 4.0%	110 9.8%	1125 100.0%

However, it is important to acknowledge that although the negative presentation of the media might cause feelings of disaffiliation to some extent, in general, British Muslims still retain strong feelings of affiliation to British society. As table 10 illustrates those who complained strongly about Islamophobic and racist coverage of the media continued to affiliate themselves to the British society. Therefore, the dissatisfaction of Muslims should be considered as a critique that comes from people who consider themselves British, and share the values of British society.

LEVEL OF RELIGIOSITY AND PERCEPTION OF MEDIA

Table 11 deals with the level of religiosity and perception of the media. According to the table, practising Muslims (70.1%) found the media to be most Islamophobic, followed by highly practising Muslims (61.1%). Alhough there is nearly a 10% gap between the two, highly practising Muslims close the percentage gap with the practising Muslims on the question of racism (17.1%) which is an offset to Islamophobia. Cultural Muslims were the ones who found the media the most racist (37.7%). Only those who did not care about Islamic values found the media fair in the greater part (40.0%). However, on the whole even they found the media representation negative (Islamophobic 40.0% and overtly fair representation and covertly destructive 20.0 %.).

Table 11: Level of Religiosity and Perception of Media

	I have no idea	Islamophobic	Racist	Fair representation of Muslims	Overtly fair representation but covertly destructive	TOTAL
I don't know	55 75.3%	14 19.2%	3 4.1%	1 1.4%	0 .0%	73 100.0%
Highly Practising Muslim	7 4.0%	107 61.1%	30 17.1%	11 6.3%	20 11.4%	175 100.0%
Practising Muslim	24 3.2%	518 70.1%	103 13.9%	21 2.8%	73 9.9%	739 100.0%
Secular Muslim	7 8.8%	36 45.0%	19 23.8%	9 11.3%	9 11.3%	80 100.0%
Cultural Muslim	0 .0%	25 47.2%	20 37.7%	1 1.9%	7 13.2%	53 100.0%
Don't care about Islamic Values at all	0 .0%	2 40.0%	0 .0%	2 40.0%	1 20.0%	5 100.0%
Total	93 8.3%	702 62.4%	175 15.6%	45 4.0%	110 9.8%	1125 100.0%

EDUCATION AND THE PERCEPTION OF MEDIA

In terms of education and perception of media, the research showed that the highest levels of dissatisfaction with the Islamophobic attitude of the media occurred in people with postgraduate level education (68.4%). Undergraduate (66.1%) and PhD (65.5%) level education levels, followed closely behind. In addition, people with PhD level education hit a very high figure (17.2%) in considering the media racist in comparison to the other two (postgraduate 11.9% and undergraduate 12.3%). If this figure is added to the figure of Islamophobia it becomes clear that people with PhD's have the most negative view regarding the media and there is an inverse correlation between the level of education and perception of the media. The higher the level to which people are educated the more dissatisfied they are. This might be due to the fact that level of education naturally increases the expectations of people. If these expectations are not fulfilled the disappointment is greater.

On the other hand, people with GCSE or equivalent level education were the least dissatisfied (53.6%) with Islamophobic coverage in the media. This is probably because they diverted their attention to another form of Islamophobia that is manifested in the form of racism. Respondents with GCSE or equivalent level education held the highest figure (22.7%) in terms of perceiving the media as being racist. One should bear in mind that racism which targets Muslims mostly takes place by identifying a particular race with Islam. For instance, throughout history, ignoring the fact that there are many non-Muslim Arabs residing in the Middle East, Arabs have been considered as being entirely Muslim. Therefore, the Arab race became equivalent to the creed of Islam. Due to this identification the Arabs, including non-Muslims faced racism that in fact targeted their Islamic identity. A similar experience was suffered by Pakistanis. Since the majority of Pakistanis are Muslim and they are identified as such, it is often the case that the racism they face is due to their religion.

Table 12:	Educational Level and perception of Media					
	I have no idea	Islamophobic	Racist	Fair representation of Muslims	Overtly fair representation but covertly destructive	TOTAL
Below GCSE	8 19.0%	23 54.8%	7 16.7%	2 4.8%	2 4.8%	42 100.0%
GCSE or Equivalent	23 10.9%	13 53.6%	48 22.7%	9 4.3%	18 8.5%	211 100.0%
A Level or Equivalent	17 7.1%	143 59.3%	42 17.4%	15 6.2%	24 10.0%	241 100.0%
Undergraduate	26 7.8%	220 66.1%	41 12.3%	7 2.1%	39 11.7%	333 100.0%
Postgraduate	18 6.7%	184 68.4%	32 11.9%	10 3.7%	25 9.3%	269 100.0%
PhD	1 3.4%	19 65.5%	5 17.2%	2 6.9%	2 6.9%	29 100.0%
Total	93 8.3%	702 62.4%	175 15.6%	45 4.0%	110 9.8%	1125 100.0%

As for reporting of issues involving Muslims in Britain the respondents held the opinion that the reports are selective, biased, stereotypical and inaccurate. Further, they confuse Islam and actions of Muslims, thus blaming Islam or all the Muslims for the actions of an individual Muslim or group.

Moreover, the media generally considers Muslims as 'others/outsiders' regardless of their being British or how much they contribute to the community. Consequently, they are blamed for anything that goes wrong, unless as a 46 year old male respondent from Bradford states "you have lost your religion and adopted the Western culture wholeheartedly":

> Issues relating to Muslims are reported with a bias outlook. Tariq Ramadan was named a radical scholar initially and eventually he was cleared. The media reports false stories regarding Muslims but once the story has been published 'MUD STICKS'.
> (Female, 22, London)

> We are represented as the "minority" and outsiders
> When we try and just practice our own religion, we are "fanatics"
> Not enough issues are related on what Islam is about or what we are about.
> (Female, 21, London)

> Poorly! Muslims (Loose term) are responsible for the actions and negative stereotyping is unfortunately being spread, rather than highlighting the positive aspects.

> In a bias manner – most of the things which incriminate us are widely broadcasted but where the Muslims are suffering … surprise, surprise. It's either not reported or it's shunned down and you never hear of it again.
> (Female, 23, London)

They are reported in a very biased way, as when a Muslim does something positive, they are known and acknowledged by there name but if they are in the media for the wrong reasons then they are known by their religion and not their name.

Though some attempts are made to gage a better understanding of Islam, this is still overshadowed by a few individuals who are a minority but are given the spotlight.

(Female, 22, Southall)

Muslims are made out to be bad, although they do not commit a lot of crimes, it has nothing to do with our religion
There is not enough insight into the Muslim community

(Male, 23, Nottingham)

Depending on whether it is negative or positive. Negative issues are highlighted more. Cultural and Islamic views are mixed together, which in most case looks at the negative side of the different culture.

(Male, 22, Halifax)

Out of touch, backward thinking, lower class.

(Male, 33, Batley)

REPRESENTATION OF MUSLIMS IN THE BRITISH MEDIA

In general all the respondents expressed a very pessimistic view with regard to Muslim representation in the media. They blamed the media for being unashamedly biased towards Muslims and presenting a negative image that suggests Muslims are 'backward', 'primitive', 'terrorist' and 'misogynistic' people. According to the findings, 62.4% of the respondents thought that the media is Islamophobic and 15.6% of respondents that the media is racist. A further 9.8% of them believe that the media is overtly fair but covertly destructive towards Muslims. Only 4.0% of the respondents said that the media was fair in representing the Muslims. This represents a very small proportion of respondents and should ring alarm bells in the British media.

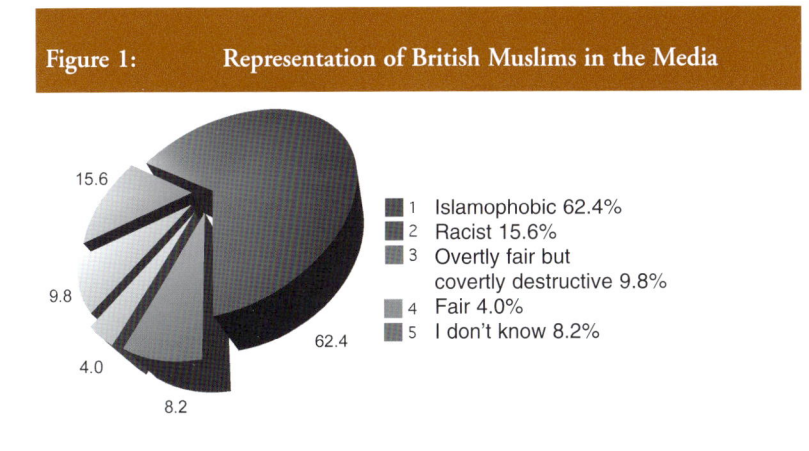

Figure 1:	Representation of British Muslims in the Media

1. Islamophobic 62.4%
2. Racist 15.6%
3. Overtly fair but covertly destructive 9.8%
4. Fair 4.0%
5. I don't know 8.2%

As already discussed, the role of the media in creating or perpetuating negative representations of Muslims does not exist in isolation from other structural forces, and is bound up in a wider discourse.

For Said (1979) the root of this negative Western perception of the East could be traced back to earlier times and has always held the idea of Western superiority over Eastern civilizations and their dark skinned people. In the beginning this superiority was considered to be an intellectual superiority. However, towards the 19th century it became an instrument by which to impose imperialist authority over the East. Moreover, these imperialist goals were justified in the Orientalist framework, since as civilized nations the West had the responsibility of bringing civilization to the primitive East.

In the 19th century the Middle East became a favorite destination for the Europeans who had a variety of reasons to visit the region. When they returned to their countries they published their observations pertaining to the region. These works were not merely their observations, however. Most had been influenced by their subconscious, fed by an existing Orientalist mind set. According to these works the native population were sometimes described in the form of exotic remnants of the past. Most often, however, they were scorned, and always regarded as uncivilized barbarians.

According to Sha'ban (1991) as a result of these publications and some other translations, e.g. *The Arabian Nights,* Western minds began to identify Arabs and Muslims from a frame of mind that imagined them as indolent, obstinate, and sensual- "wild, cruel, savages or robbers, in greater or lesser degree".

According to the account of respondents it seems that they understand the British media to have an Orientalist mindset by producing similar kinds of negative images about Muslims today:

> The way in which Islam and Muslim people are portrayed in the media is abhorrent. Muslims are portrayed as 'women repressors and limb amputators' to quote Robert Kilroy Silk's words. However, the biggest challenge is terrorism which is now tarnishing the name of Islam. The media is just glorifying the image of terrorism and Islam and associating the two in news headlines. Although this is the normal representation this approach needs change.
> (Female, 22, London)

> Very biased. Although they try to say that Muslims are law abiding citizens; however they take every opportunity to describe them as the cause of all evil in Britain today. All the new anti-human rights laws passed by the government are aimed at Muslims in all walks of life and not only at terrorists of all types of doctrines and religions.
> (Male, 43, Edinburgh)

> Misconcepted, biased, edited, judgmental, condemning
> (Male, 19, Bradford)

> Very negatively, when it comes to Islam the words of the reporters just turn sour…shame on them.
> (Female, 20, London)

> Very negatively, the full account is not given. Info and pictures are very negative.
> (Male, 20, Keighley)

> Very bad, anti-Islam, Anti-Muslim
> (Male, 35, Braford)

> Islam is represented as this very uncompromising religion that does not approve of discussion and logic and is full of contradictions, is oppressive towards women and encourages violence………Muslims are these rigid and backward, fundamentalists who have one main purpose "suicide bombing". They are portrayed as some kind of threat to the British society. Their achievements in different fields are hardly ever heard of…………programs like Panorama have only enhanced such stereotypical thoughts…..
> (Female, 30, Oldham)

> Muslims are under represented in the media, however, when the Muslims are made mention of they are demonized in such away that the public feel frightened of them. Consequently, Muslims have been and still are the subjects of bullying, harassment, victimization, intimidation, physical and verbal attacks which occur at work or whilst even walking down the street.
>
> The media's portrayal of Muslims has created much negativity and misinformation that Muslims are being pushed out of society leaving them helpless and isolated, which is due no fault of the Muslims at all.
> (Male, 25, West Midlands)

> I think they are presented in a very negative way; the media gives spotlight to a few individuals who do not represent Islam in its true form, hence portraying a very negative picture.
> (Female, 22, Southall)

> Exploited and are misguided
> (Female, 20, London)

The media seems to promote a more liberal form of Islam and categorizes many mainstream Muslims as "extremists". Religious Muslims are often given a bad image and the Shariah is grossly misrepresented.

The media covertly stigmatizes religious Muslims as being close minded, violent, backward and anti-women. They do this by constantly associating the wrong actions of some Muslims with terms such as "Islamic extremism". Liberal and irreligious Muslims are sometimes wrongly labelled as devout. This could be due the fact that the western society in general has lower standards for religiosity and also because they want Muslims to become less orthodox in their religious outlook.

The media is also at fault for not differentiating the cultural practices of Muslims from the truth of their religion. A lot of times Islam is not judged according to its teachings but by the actions of its supposed followers.

The achievements of Muslims and the benefits of Islam on society are hardly ever reported.

> Certainly negative, often the 'key suspects' in major crimes. People who are disorganized and disorientated and often unrepresented.
> (Male, 20, London)

A few of the respondents expressed mixed feelings and argued that though there are some negative representations of Muslims, the media is sometimes fair in representing them. However, they complained that fair and constructive programmes are mostly scheduled in the late hours, thus, making it an arduous task to watch them:

> I feel there can be a very skewed representation via the news and the general perception of the Muslims is that of negative portrayals. However, there are also positive and accurate programs and media, but sometimes these are shown at unusual hours. A typical example is the excellent "Mosque" program on ITV- it is factually correct and shows the correct good image of Islam and Muslims but is shown at 12.10 am on a Sunday night/Monday morning! I have worked with BBC Radio Kent on a number of occasions and they have put together interviews which portray Muslims in a good light.
> (Male, 35, Gillingham)

> Mixed. Sometimes good, sometimes very negative and hostile e.g. on Islamic extreme groups - 'horizon' but also by Muslims presenters, they give good depth to a story but not always much on what Islam may say on a subject.
> (Female, 20, Lincoln)

PORTRAYAL OF BRITISH MUSLIMS AND NON-BRITISH MUSLIMS

The interviews suggested that there is no significant distinction in reporting the issues that describes Muslims in Britain and in Muslim or other countries. According to the respondents' accounts the media employ the same mindset and portray the same image. However, a few of the respondents think that media is more ruthless in portraying the Muslims who live in Muslim countries since they are not able to raise their voice:

> I think they are generally biased and inaccurate- the often paint half a picture and the result is that the average person who has no knowledge of the history of the situation or the issues surrounding the situation can draw incorrect conclusions.
> (Male, 35, Gillingham)

Always show a biased point of view, they take incidents and points out of context and present wrong messages.

(Female, 24, London)

> Disturbing images of political, social and economic unrest that conveys the persecution of Muslims by their own so called "leaders". There seems to be a lack of cohesive understanding that creates an image of savage and backwardness.
> (Male)

> Muslim countries generally that have been reported are generally of the same category……..they all seem to be either terrorists themselves so harboring terrorism…hardly ever anything positive or exciting is reported about Muslims in these Muslim countries….
> (Female, 30, Oldham)

Once again, I feel the media is very selective, and more often than not, describes negative issues or events that have occurred which may be due to several reasons such as feuds over land, money, pride etc..., but connivingly links this to religion and Islam. Infamous examples include terrorist acts with Muslims alleged as ' Islamic Terrorists', whereas in Ireland terrorists fighting over religion is merely portrayed in a political sense. Less obvious examples include family honor killings being supposedly justified by perpetrators as related to Islam.

(Male, 18, London)

Can be negative, like they support a certain person strongly, who the rest of the world see as a terrorist. e.g. a documentary on Saudi Arabia and some people were supportive of e.g. Osama Bin Laden, it can paint all Muslims with one brush.

(Female, 20, Lincoln)

Sometimes you get the feeling that when watching a programme about Muslims in Muslim countries, the aim of the programme is to frighten the viewer or defame the Islamic religion and culture. Rare are programmes where Islam is reflected positively and truly.

(Male, 43, Edinburgh)

Backward people, In need of liberalization, Violent to women, Violent to non-Muslims living in those countries.

(Male, 20, London)

Unfairly a Muslim does something wrong and Islam is the one that goes on trial. However, when Muslims achieve or are the cries being persecuted, then the spotlight ceases to exist and these issues are pushed under the rug. However, when they see Muslims pushing the idea of integration into British society i.e. 'British and Muslim' then they report on this as if it's the best way to go i.e. they're happy with Muslims and Islam only if we compromise our *deen*.

(Female, 19, Nottingham)

Muslims living in Muslim countries are given a very distorted image by the media. I believe they are given a much worse image than those living here because the media can get away with it. Those Muslims cannot put any real pressure on the media and the British public is very much unaware of the reality in Muslims countries. Thus the media can give the public a negative image of those countries without the public being able to verify it for themselves. This negative image is given to Muslim countries more than any other group of nations even though the others may be suffering from even worse problems. Any negative aspects of Muslim countries are severely amplified by the media.

Muslim countries are portrayed as being backward and repressive. Their culture and leaders are vilified and the more Islamic nations such as Iran are given an even more ridiculously distorted image.

(Male, 25, London)

Generally, very negatively. Although the Muslims in Britain are portrayed in a slightly more positive light, it is easier for the media to portray non-British Muslims negatively, as the reaction is strong, as it is often not themselves being targeted. This is true I believe on a general level.

(Male, 20, Manchester)

ISLAMOPHOBIA IN HOLLYWOOD AND BRITISH MOVIES:

Hollywood has played a major role in the negative portrayal of Muslims. Movies commanding huge budgets and human resources to influence the masses depict Islam in a horrific manner. These movies perhaps caused the most damage to the image of Islam in the West because of their tremendous influence.

In fact, anti-Arabic/Islamic sentiment parallel to that existing in Europe had already developed in the U.S., and American public and intellectuals were already familiar with the Orientalist mindset. The Orientalist European perception that was shaped in the 19th century was adopted by the U.S. intelligentsia. As the nineteenth century went on U.S. writers began to challenge Islam directly, writing about the religion and the Prophet Muhammad for the explicit purpose of exposing Islam as a "heap of rubbish," a fraud, and the Prophet Muhammad as an 'evil schemer' (Christison, 2001). Hollywood did not have much difficulty in adapting itself to this discourse.

The accounts of the respondents indicate that the negative portrayal of Muslims is heavily presented in the films that are produced in both the UK and US. In the movies Muslims are mostly portrayed as terrorists who randomly kill people (usually innocents) or blow things up -including themselves-, or as hijackers, misogynistic or stupid who cannot achieve anything and are therefore in need of continuous supervision. Some respondents believe that the film industry is used as a tool in the foreign policy of Western countries in terms of demonizing and gaining public support against a fashioned enemy. For Chomsky that was the reason why Churchill established a government propaganda commission during the First World War, called the Creel Commission. The commission was so successful that within six months it had turned "a pacifist population into a hysterical, warmongering population which wanted to destroy everything German, tear the Germans limb from limb, go to war and save the world." The admitted aim of this commission was not only to control the British public but "to control the thought of the world." (Chomsky: 1993, p. 23). Therefore, in order to agitate the feelings of masses and gear them up for war the Commission fabricated great atrocities and terrible incidents. Chomsky argues further that it was the British propaganda machine that dragged US public and intellectuals into the war.

In the Cold War era, it was the USSR which was targeted by the handy propaganda machine and many anti-Soviet movies were produced by western film industries, especially by Hollywood. After the collapse of the USSR, some respondents believe Islam and Muslims became the chief enemy and was heavily targeted by Western filmmakers. In support of this argument Said (1997) argued that the collapse of the Soviet Union was a major reason for the anti-Muslim propaganda in the media. This was due to the change in perception of the threat to western states.

> The portrayal is extremely negative, I believe of Islam, Muslims and Arabs. Stereotyping is more common than ever and an Arab in a Hollywood film is almost exclusively represented as a terrorist. Many British spy dramas on television also contain this stereotyping, such as Spooks.
>
> (Male, 20, Manchester)

> Usually antagonists – 'bad guys' – Kingdom of Heaven
>
> (Female, 18, London)

> Hollywood and Bollywood always portrays Muslims negatively – as fanatics and criminals.
>
> (Female, 23, Bow, London)

In TV on those BBC dramas (spooks I think) there was the story of the terrorist guy planning to bomb some place.

(Female, 20, London)

There was this film where they showed a Muslim planning to blow himself up and he went to make Wudhu [ablution] before that.

They often make films showing CIA how intelligent they are and how they found nuclear weapons in Iran (as if they don't have any). (Female, 21, London)

Certainly the new "enemy" are the Muslims. This was seen clearly in True Lies (Arnold Schwarzenegger) and is seen in many comedies as well as older classic films. Muslims are often portrayed as either ignorant, stupid, slave types or terrorists.

(Male, 35, Gillingham)

Portrayal of Islam is totally negative, Muslims are terrorists, always blowing things up, and women are oppressed with their Hijab on. In general, the images are negative.

(Female, 24, London)

I am often disappointed at the portrayal of Muslims in films, and there are many examples large and small. I can't think of any of the top of my head, but any that portray Muslims as terrorists, woman oppressors and so on.

(Male, 20, London)

Very negative & progressively more so. Shown as backward, savage and who need to be freed to live western lifestyles

(Male, 23, Nottingham)

Often as the bad guy, the terrorist

(Male, 21, Nottingham)

Negative, films – True Lies – Muslims are portrayed as terrorists and get killed in the end

(Male, 25, Bradford)

Really bad examples are 'True Lies' and 'East is East'

(Male, 45, Liverpool)

Stereotype, Anti Islamic, Anti Arab, Need a new boogey man after the collapse of communism e.g. Soviet Union.

(Male, 35, Bradford)

I can't think of any examples at hand. However, I think the general stereotypes are that Arabs and/or Muslims are terrorists often responsible for kidnapping and hijacking. (Male, 18, London)
Always negative.

(Female, 20, England)

Very extreme, their used as terrorist in films, which portrays the wrong image.

(Male, 20, Keighley)

Very extreme, their used as terrorist in films, which portrays the wrong image.

(Male, 20, Keighley)

> I don't personally trust any films, but the way I see it is that Muslims and Arabs are shown as backward, killers and stupid people.
> (Male, 20, Nottingham)

A few suggest that the negative portrayal of Muslims and Islam is the product of 9/11 and in the past it was possible to see some Hollywood movies that were sympathetic towards Muslim:

> Hollywood is overtly anti Islam since 9/11 however earlier it was quite understanding and even accepting Islam. Rambo III or II was about the war against the Afghans and Russians… the funny thing is that Muslims were shown as good allies in this film. Another film would be Robin Hood Prince of Thieves in which Morgan Freeman plays a Moor (Spanish Muslim) who prays east and is a faithful sidekick to Kevin Costner who plays Robin Hood. This film is an early 1990s production. Having looked just at these examples it's possible to see there were some good depictions of Islam however all traces of this cease to exist. Bollywood has also produced a few films depicting Muslims as terrorists (Loc and Fiza).
> (Female, 22, London)

However, it should be noted that where Muslim characters have appeared in films they have been extremely popular. In the 1980s when the Muslim character, whose name was Nasir, was first played in the British TV series of *Robin of Sherwood*, he played the role of a servant of the evil sorcerer Simon De Belleme, brought back from the Crusades. Nasir was supposed to have been killed in the early episodes of the series. But the character became so popular that the producer of the series decided to continue with him. Nasir joined Robin and his gang and was integral to the fight against injustice. This early Muslim character was recreated in later versions of Robin Hood and presented a positive image of Muslims (Abdelmoteleb, 2006).

DIFFERENT REPRESENTATIONS IN THE DIFFERENT FORMS OF MEDIA

VISUAL MEDIA

There are different opinions among respondents regarding the differences in representations between the different forms of media. Some suggest that TV is better than other forms of media since the audience is able to examine the given evidence with its own eyes.

> People usually believe television more because there is evidence
> (Female, 20, London)

AUDITORY MEDIA

On the other hand, some believes that auditory media is less harmful than visual media since using images in the wrong context could be far more manipulative.

> Absolutely. The damage done by radio stations is limited because they have no visual aid. Given so, I often find less bad portrayals of Islam by channels such as the BBC World/ BBC News, than channels owned by Rupert Murdoch (e.g. Fox News, Sky News etc.)
> (Male, 18, London)

> There are very little differences in my opinion although when things are written on the internet there is more care taken opposed to what is said by reporters. The form of radio is probably less dangerous to the Islamic image because there are no images or imagery and these tend to be the form in which most viewers are taken in.
> (Female, 22, London)

THE INTERNET

Some respondents held the view that because of its wider range of choices the Internet is the most reliable source of information. However others accused the Internet as being the chief perpetrator of Islamophobia in the media.

> TV and radio programmes are biased. Programmes are done from the point of view of the producer or the presenter which is always subjective. However, the internet offers a varied set of choice and websites that express hatred for Islam and Muslims so not hide their feelings.
> (Male, 43, Edinburgh)

> There is hardly any differences in papers, radio, TV and satellite channels. The only media one can say has a certain amount of truth is the internet but you have to find the 'right sites'
> (Male, 35, Braford)

> It's surprising to see that because the internet can show varied forms of the news, I believe it to be more truthful as there is always more than one side of an argument. As TV is visual and very mainstream, there are restrictions on what can or can't be shown.
> (Male, 19, Bradford)

> The Internet contains the most controversial and negative views of Islam, given the medium and the ease of contributing to it. As mentioned above, Channel 4 is the most objective in its representations. The BBC is also objective but there have been occurrences of misrepresentations.
> (Male, 20, Oldham)

Overall, the majority believe that though there are differences in forms of media, these variations are insignificant and in general they present the same negative image of Muslims:

> Not really, at the end of the day, they represent the people owning them.
> (Male, 20, Nottingham)

> Similarly, an attempt to be unbiased but always ends on a negative note.
> (Female, 27, London)

> Depends on what they are reporting. Generally I don't think that there is much of a difference.
> (Female, 25)

> No, there are no differences in the representation.
> (Female, 21, Batley)

> Very little amongst non Muslims. Channel Four is less biased but all other media home in on this viewpoint.
>
> (Female, 27, London)

> Not really
>
> (Female, 20, England)

> No they are all the same
>
> (Male, 45, Liverpool)

> None. They are always extreme in their views
>
> (Male, 30, Bradford)

> No
>
> (Female, 22, Birmingham)

> All the same
>
> (Female, 28, Bradford)

> None.
>
> (Male, 25, Bradford)

Having acknowledged the unreliability of the mainstream media, interestingly, some of the respondents do not tend to alternative media sources that are available.

> No! I don't like the media
> They are biased and use of language is always against Muslims.
>
> (Female, 21, London)

> No.
>
> (Male, 45, Liverpool)

> No.
>
> (Male, 20, London)

> Not really
>
> (Male, 21, Nottingham)

Some followed alternative media where they think they can acquire more reliable information and those who opt to find an alternative mostly follow the Islamic media.

> Always – Islamic media in specific – because we get a wider picture rather than a selective one.
>
> (Female, 18, London)

> I tend to read Muslim Weekly or other Muslim websites. I've even resorted to whatreallyhappened.com because of fear that most news is slandering Muslims.
>
> (Female, 22, London)

> Use Muslim websites to further the mainstream media & read news approved by them
>
> (Male, 23, Nottingham)

> Yes. Muslim channels (Islam Channel/ARY/PTV/Geo etc). To acknowledge and gain a different perspective.
>
> (Male)

Further, some respondents considered non-Islamic media as alternative media and followed them:

> I like the Channel 4 News when I watch it. It gets right to the heart of issues.
> (Female, 22, Edinburgh)

> BBC news website, The Guardian, The Times
> (Male, 20, Nottingham)

Some respondents used both Muslim and non-Muslim media:

> Islam Channel, Muslim Weekly and Emel magazine. Websites such as Islam way and BBC World News.
> (Female, 23, Bow, London)

The findings show a great distrust for mainstream media which diverts Muslims to alternative media. One explanation for this can be found in the failure of the mainstream media to properly represent minorities. As Baer (1998) explains in the framework of 'muted group theory', a male dominated society silences and controls women. According to her view the dominant group shapes the rules, roles, relations, perception of the world and even very structure of the society and dictates the controlled members to behave accordingly. That includes language and the words that describe the dominant group and controlled group(s). Through this process of silencing the controlled group(s), the dominant group can sustain its power.

The same theory is very much applicable to the Muslims who are silenced by the majority who set their values and try to impose them upon Muslims without any negotiation. This process of silencing causes great consternation among Muslims and leads them to alternative media where they can express themselves freely.

COMPLAINTS AND RESPONSES

Another interesting finding of the interviews is that most of those who are distressed with the negative portrayal of Muslims in the media showed no interest in complaining about them. When they are asked why their answers highlight their alienation from society.

> Sadly enough I never have………… basically because I don't think I would actually get any kind of response…..
> (Female, 30, Oldham)

> No what's the point
> (Female, 28, Bradford)

> No, I did not because I thought it would not make any difference or they would not listen.
> (Male, 35, Bradford)

> No. You are right Muslims should do. Unfortunately, like a proper slacker, turn off the TV.
> (Male)

> Unfortunately no, will do in the future if need be inshAllah.
> (Female, 24, London)

The accounts of those who did complain about the negative portrayals support the pessimism of those who have never made any complaint. Almost all of them failed to get a response.

> No use – nothing's ever done. Complained ages ago about a programme on channel 4 which portrayed Islam in a negative way – heard nothing about it.
>
> (Female, 23, London)

> I complained about the 9/11 documentary on BBC but did not receive any response.
>
> (Female, 23, Bow, London)

> Emailed concerning reports in news report which were misleading and wrong. No reply.
>
> (Male, 22, Halifax)

> Yes – channel 4, Marie Claire
>
> (Female, 18, London)

> Yes T&A Bradford
>
> No response
>
> (Male, 25, Bradford)

> I have complained about newspaper articles but never got any return communications.
>
> (Male, 35, Gillingham)

> No response.
>
> (Female, 21, London)

IDEOLOGICAL REPRESENTATION: ENCODED MESSAGES ABOUT MUSLIMS

According to Amin (1989), it was western imperial and colonial ambitions that shaped the image of Muslims and Islam in the minds of Western people. For Amin the idea of western superiority over the rest of the world came into existence by the realization of the fact that European civilization has the potential of conquering the world. This realization took place during the period of Renaissance through the Enlightenment. This realization was the result or process of the capitalist mode of organization of European society. He names this period as the 'crystallization of the Eurocentric' worldview.

Amin (1988), therefore, adamantly refuses Said's approach, though he agrees with the findings of Said. In his book wherein he promotes his Eurocentric theory, Amin draws attention to the fact that the frame of mind that presumes European superiority over the East was shaped in modern times:

> "During the Crusades, Christians, and Moslems each believed themselves to be keepers of the superior religious faith, but at this stage of their evolution, as evidence has proven, neither one was capable of imposing its global vision on the other. That is why the judgments of the Christians at the time of the Crusaders are no more "Eurocentric" than those of the Moslems are "Islamocentric." Dante relegated Mohamed to Hell but it was not a sign of a Eurocentric conception of the world, contrary to what Edward Said

has suggested. It is only a case of banal provincialism, which is something quite different, because it is symmetrical in the minds of two opposing parties." (Amin: 1989, p.74)

From Amin's point of view this realization process created a mythical idea of an "'eternal West' unique since the moment of its origin" (Amin: 1989, p.89). Consequently, this artificial idea gave rise to its counterpart concept namely the 'Other' (s) (the "Orients" or "the Orient). In order to, legitimize this theory, European history was rewritten through the sieve of a Eurocentric vision that suggested it was unique in terms of its progressive and stable trajectory. This route progressed from Ancient Greece to Rome to feudal Christian Europe to capitalist Europe.

Conversely, the East was lacking this stable progress, needed the support of a superior civilization empowered with a capitalist system, and had to overcome its primitive, dark, unprogressive and threatening nature that was inimical to Western values and ideals.

Most of the respondents concurred with Amin's theory and approached the issue from an ideological point of view. According to their views, Islam is the fastest growing religion in the world and this fact is worrying the capitalist West since this would diminish Western hegemony. Yet, some held the idea that the reason was fear fuelled by ignorance. Since the Western public is ignorant of Islam, consequently it is also afraid of it.

> The media portrays Islam in the way that it does out of fear that Islam is growing. The race for oil and the worry that the values of Islam are anti capitalist is especially worrying for the West as it breaks their dreams of being money grabbing superpowers. Islam is feared for the truth that it holds and for many agnostic and atheist people there is fear that Islam is the true religion.
> (Female, 22, London)

> This is because the ideology of the west conflicts with the teaching of Islam and with more people reverting to Islam there is a fear hence they try to portray Islam in a negative way
> (Female, 22, Southall)

> They are afraid of the truth and just causes that Islam stands for. Islam stands against oppression, capitalism and totalitarianism.
> (Female, 23, Bow, London)

> Because they don't understand what Islam truly is and they hate Islam. American propaganda is the cause of their hate towards us. Behind American propaganda are the yahood (Jews) because they know who are actually the Muslims, they seek to destroy us Muslims (the Zionists) because they are cowards and afraid of all Arab countries surrounding and supporting Palestine, the land they claim is theirs.
> (Female, 21, London)

> Because they are ignorant of Islam. Afraid that the principles of Islam will dominate their lives and the world at large. Some know the truth about Islam but don't want to admit it.
> Fear, hatred and jealousy, also lack of understanding
> (Male, 27, Bradford)

Some suggest that it is a government policy to create an enemy through which they can strengthen their position and control the public. Further, a few respondents blame Muslim extremists and their actions for the negative portrayal of Muslims in the media:

> We are the new enemy. "Back in the day" it was Communism, then Hitler, then the Japanese…we have been portrayed as evil or ignorant people. This is because of our own actions partly and because of the way leaders want us to be portrayed.
> (Male, 35, Gillingham)

> Because of the wrong portrayals that extremists give out.
> Because of recent events – July bombings, Iraq War, 9/11, The Taleban – Osama Bin Laden (who conveniently disappears when the American government have too much to deal with), Palestine … I can go on.
> (Female, 20, London)

> Because they are ignorant and uncivilized people who have no real knowledge of the beautiful and humble religion decreed by Allah all mighty.
>
> Allah Guides whom he pleases
> (Female, 21, London)

> It appears that they are trying to destroy the image of Islam. The government also seems to be using the media to its own advantage as well. By demonizing Islam and instilling fear into the masses it has and is continuing to push forward unjust and discriminatory laws e.g. 'anti-terrorism laws', and its agenda.
> (Male, 25, West Midlands)

PHOBIC REPRESENTATION OF MUSLIMS: INTERCULTURAL CONSEQUENCES

Islamophobia has at least three important consequences: first it creates a structural fear for all members of society including non-Muslims. This environment will make life insecure for both Muslims and non-Muslims. Secondly it will intensify tension and anxiety in intercultural relationships between Muslims and others. The most important consequence will appear on internal and international policy for legitimizing war against Muslims.

Many think that the current media portrayal of Muslims has a very negative effect on British Muslims. Intensive media propaganda against Muslims makes them further alienated from and by society. Furthermore, it leaves deep physiological damage on Muslims who face constant Islamophobic elements in their daily life i.e. verbal and physical assault, humiliation, discrimination (Ameli *et al* 2004b). The link between media portrayal and negative daily experience is a recurrent theme in this project with Muslim schoolchildren stating that they expected the government to tackle the media as the main way their educational aspirations could be met (Ameli *et al*, 2005). In this volume's research some respondents also felt that Muslim youth suffered most from Islamophobic propaganda in the media. It causes distrust and frustration towards the media and consequently society, making them vulnerable to extremist ideas and groups. Thus, it would be appropriate to argue that the irresponsibility of the media is one of the major barriers to a stable and peaceful society that people want to live in, in Britain. The media harbours and instigates hatred and animosity against Muslims; this feeds the extremism that we witnesses today.

Negative impact only way people know/learn/get more information about Muslims – so it's restrictive.

(Female, 18, London)

It influences their beliefs about state of affairs, their opinions. Their behavior - they try to accommodate/ compromise.

(Female, 27, London)

Especially, in regards to the youth they have no role models to look up to. Also lies and wrong information that is shown in mainstream media, frustrates the youth as they feel there is no justice and truth in media.

(Female, 23, Bow, London)

The Muslims are attacked by such media representation and are oppressed by British society and subjected to Islamophobia both physically and verbally. Muslims are treated less importantly and also they are feared and hated as a result. The Muslims in particular may find it difficult to get jobs or work or even attend school/college/university.

(Female, 22, London)

It has many impacts. Those with little knowledge of Islam tend to believe what is presented by the media. People become passive in practicing their religion.

(Female, 24, London)

We feel ostracized, but if Muslims are proud and practice their religion we will stand united regardless. Allah is the Protector and has the best of plans.

(Female, 21, London)

Muslims have directly been stereotyped as "fundamental terrorist". It's also affected how a Muslim looks e.g. a man with a beard can be considered as an extremist/terrorist.

(Male, 19, Bradford)

On the other hand, a few respondents argued that although the current Muslim portrayal in the media has many negative effects on Muslims i.e. force them to compromise their religion with the aim of becoming less devout Muslims, these negative portrayals raise curiosity or a sense of identity among Muslims and eventually drive them to become more practising:

It can have both positive and negative impact, positive in the sense that it leaves a curiosity about Islam in the minds of Muslim and when they read or look more in to it they become more practicing and negative in the sense that it becomes hard to practice Islam as there is a fear of being labeled as an extremist.

(Female, 22, London)

A lot. It makes the Muslims more inclined to Islam. It doesn't matter how practising you are, as soon as Islam is put under attack, the Muslims will defend Islam. In that sense it has made some Muslims act on their emotion, but on the other hand, a lot more Muslims are starting to think, use their initiative to create their own media etc. etc. as they know you can only combat thought with thought.

(Female, 19, Nottingham)

IMPACTS ON NON-MUSLIMS

As for the impact of the negative representation of the media on non-Muslims, respondents unanimously believed that it had a deleterious effect. They considered the media as a primary education tool, since everybody (especially the youth) spent considerable time using it in their daily lives. The presentation that radiates from the media shapes the thoughts of non-Muslims in a negative manner. They consider Islam as a backward, savage and uncivilized religion. As a result they develop anti-Islamic sentiments and this is reflected -overtly or covertly- in their relations with and attitudes towards the Muslims in this country. In conclusion, the negative presentation of Muslims by the media causes profound polarization and conflict in British society.

However, its impact can be self-confirming for Muslims. Negative propaganda raises curiosity among some non-Muslims about Islam and leads them to become more practising.

The non-Muslim public in general gets its knowledge about Islam and Muslims from the mass media. The negative image given by the media results in Muslims being discriminated by those people who may be inclined towards religious and racial prejudice. As a result of the media coverage of the London bombings, Muslims have suffered form physical and verbal abuse. There cannot be any doubt that Muslims are also victims in the job market and are less likely to get jobs.

> Many Muslims have taken up a cautious and apologetic attitude towards the media coverage. Some have decided to abandon the religious attire for their own safety. However this negative media coverage may be a blessing in disguise because Islam is in the limelight and it gives Muslims the opportunity to do *dawah* and spread the truth about their religion to a more interested western audience.
> (Male, 25, London)

> Although many non-Muslims, certainly in Britain, are taught to respect Islam and other religions when younger and may have Muslim friends, it seems that the media is their main education on Islam and Muslims. As a result, I think this is where the media's negative representation does most damage. Despite that, a positive outcome is the significant interest in Islam that it creates (especially after 9/11) which *inshAllah* can lead to more non-Muslims reverting to Islam.
> (Male, 18, London

> I think not everyone but a big section of non Muslims do see Muslims and Islam as very rigid and very violent …… not very social and welcoming Islamic people…. It creates a very Islamophobic feeling amongst non Muslims.
> (Male, 20, Manchester)

> Don't understand the real meaning of the religion.
> (Female, 20, London)

> A very bad and negative effect leading to racial abuse and attacks
> (Female, 20, London)

> Some non–Muslims as a result perceive Islam as an oppressive religion which undermines women, is too strict and breeds terrorism. These views are particularly enforced by the media.
> (Female, 22, London)

We have to remember that the average person in Britain who day in day out only ever sees Muslims of hears the name of Islam when it is related to killing innocents, suicide bombing, Osama bin Laden etc is going to get a biased opinion from it. It doesn't necessarily mean they will hate all Muslims but it will affect their judgment and until they see the real full story or meet real Muslims or see what Islam is really about they will carry this bias.

This can result in being viewed negatively without being even given the chance to explain and having an uphill struggle to be seen as an equal. It can obviously result in verbal and physical attacks and job refusals etc.

(Male, 35, Gillingham)

They perceive Islam as a horrible religion but when they actually go to search about Islam they actually convert.

(Female, 21, London)

A bad effect, non-Muslims are not interested in Islam in a positive way

(Male, 25, Bradford)

Non-Muslims think Islam is a backward, evil religion

(Male, 30, Bradford)

RESPONSIBILITY OF MEDIA REGARDING ISLAMOPHOBIA

When the respondents were asked about the role of the media that they play in inter-faith and inter-community relations the respondents noticeably expressed their discontent regarding the role of the media. They initially acknowledged the leading role of the media in inter-faith and inter-community relations; however, they came to the conclusion that media somehow abuses this role and widens already existing divisions. It seems the Muslim community has greatly suffered from misrepresentation by the media and this has left little room for any positive feelings:

> The media has played a massive role in causing divides and stirring up racial hatred, it is without a doubt that the media is propagating lies and misinformation in regard to Islam and the Muslims.
>
> (Male, 25, West Midlands)

The media has one of the biggest roles and they abuse that.

(Female, 21, London)

They should be at the forefront of such a notion but often are not.

(Male, 20, London)

They give us a lot to talk about!
Many of the misconceptions are fuelled by the media. They don't look at the relations between the people of the book
Very important effect on intercommunity relations i.e. greater hostility, and low willingness to discuss

(Male, 23, Nottingham

> I feel this is where the media does most damage. The fine line is that it points between political and social issues, in relation to more narrowly religious issues, can often hinder, it seems co-operating with individuals who are Muslims or deal with Muslims.
> (Male, 18, London)

> None, only hatred
> (Male, 20, Bradford)

> Very little role
> (Male, 27, Bradford)

> Non existent
> (Female, 22, Birmingham)

> Does tackle by making it worse
> (Male, 45, Liverpool)

Only one respondent had faith in the media:

> Local papers are quite good at promoting events in the area of an interfaith nature. The broadsheets are quite good as well as sometimes art promoting national events.
> (Female, 22, Edinburgh)

All the respondents unanimously pointed to the media as being the chief instrument of Islamophobia. Respondents argued that the media explicitly or implicitly damaged the name of Islam and Muslims. In coverage of issues concerning Muslims some words i.e. terrorism, bombing, hijacking, extremism, are deliberately inserted. Hence, they manipulate people to believe that all Muslims are related or are supporters of these activities. In this respect, Minority Rights Group International has concluded that "'the media's portrayal portrayal and representation of Islam has been one of the most prevalent, virulent and socially significant sources of Islamophobia in Britain." (Ansari, 2002 p. 24)

> Yes, because of the bad portrayal that non Muslims fear the religion.
> (Female, 20, London)

> Yes!!!
> (Female, 20, London)

> They are responsible for most of the problems e.g. Islamophobia
> (Male, 35, Bradford)

> Hell yeah!!! Media is responsible indirectly and directly for breeding Islamophobia. They play with words and ideas (Islamic extremists, Muslim fundamentalist, Islamic militants). These words have become quite common in the English language and are on the tips of most people's tongues.
> (Female, 22, London)

> Yes definitely! (London Bombings) of UK and USA. USA television always mention "September 11 attacks" when describing dates e.g. instead of saying so and so happened on 11 September, they'd say "so and so happened 2 months just after the 9/11 attacks". In UK – in all bus stops and train stations – posters "if you see anything suspicious…"
> (Female, 21, London)

> Yes of course, there are many cases of irresponsible media portrayals.
> (Male, 20, London)

> Yes totally
> (Male, 25, Bradford)

> Yes it is, if they portrayed Islam in a positive light, then people would not fear us
> (Male, 30, Bradford)

> Media tends to sensationalize stories which can lead to an exaggeration of people's emotions.
> (Female, 22, Edinburgh)

> It is origin of Islamophobia. They have planted it, they are nurturing it and causing it to appear as an ogre.
> (Male, 43, Edinburgh)

> Yes, in some ways.
> (Male, 20, Nottingham)

In view of the above discussion respondents who have experienced anti-Islamic sentiments blamed the media and its negative representation of Muslims. In fact, one female Muslim stated that since she did not wear Islamic clothing she was able avoid these sentiments whereas another respondent who dressed in Islamic clothes was subjected to anti-Islamic sentiments. These statements are very important in terms of understanding the effect of negative presentation of the Muslims in the media. Since the media has often portrayed Islamic clothing as a symbol of fanaticism those who harboured anti-Islamic sentiments targeted these symbols. Thus, Muslims who merely wanted to practise their religion suffered greatly:

> Especially after July 7, 2005 - stares, being pushed and verbally assaulted. I blame this on the negative image portrayed by media – especially The Sun, Express, Evening Standard, and Daily Mail
> (Female, 23, Bow, London)

> Yes the September 11 attacks and July 7, 2005 attacks have led to some feelings of hatred towards Muslims and I have born some of the brunt as many other Muslims through verbal abuse. The media representation has played the most part in the form of trashy tabloid THE SUN. This newspaper has defamed Muslims for a number of years now and is obviously of a Zionist nature which is why it plays the role of representing Muslims.
> (Female, 22, London)

> Well me personally no, but I believe I would if I wore headscarf. My friends at college who do veil experience a lot of discrimination from a specific teacher who is Arab but Anti Islamic. It is all linked to American and UK propaganda.
> (Female, 21, London)

> Yes, I wear clothing in accordance with the *sunnah* and non-Muslims call me Taliban, and Osama bin laden
> (Male, 25, Bradford)

> I deal with anti-Islamic sentiments on almost a daily basis and yes, I do believe the media is a huge contributor to this due to its misrepresentation of Islam.
> (Male, 25, West Midlands)

Common people, and they represent the majority of the British population, don't try to use objective judgment in analyzing facts. They jump into conclusions and react in a negative, spontaneous way. I personally have experienced many instances of intimidation and racist name-calling since the London bombings.

(Male,43, Edinburgh)

Table 13 further elaborates the relation between anti-Islamic sentiments and perception of the media. Those who have experienced Islamophobia on daily (74.7%), weekly (80.2%), monthly (70.1%) bases and only occasionally (65.1%) held the media responsible for the anti-Islamic sentiments that they have faced. This could be due to their perception of how negative media coverage can influence people and lead them to behave in a destructive way.

Table 13:	Discrimination and Perception of Media					
	I have no idea	Islamophobic	Racist	Fair representation of Muslims	Overtly fair representation but covertly destructive	TOTAL
I don't Know	56 86.2%	7 10.8%	2 3.1%	0 .0%	0 .0%	65 100.0%
Almost Daily	1 1.1%	68 74.7%	20 22.0%	0 .0%	2 2.2%	91 100.0%
Weekly	2 2.2%	73 80.2%	12 13.2%	1 1.1%	3 3.3%	91 100.0%
Monthly	4 4.6%	61 70.1%	15 17.2%	1 1.1%	6 6.9%	87 100.0%
Only on some occasion	23 3.7%	404 65.1%	97 15.6%	20 3.2%	77 12.4%	621 100.0%
Not at all	7 4.1%	89 52.4%	29 17.1%	23 13.5%	22 12.9%	170 100.0%
Total	93 8.3%	702 62.4%	175 15.6%	45 4.0%	110 9.8%	1125 100.0%

DOES THE MEDIA GIVE ENOUGH OPPORTUNITY TO MUSLIMS?

Many respondents believe that the media did not give enough opportunity to Muslims to represent themselves. Even though there are some Muslim figures who appear in the media they are the ones who held extremist views or are marginalized Muslims who do not represent the Muslim community at all. Ansari (2003) expressed his concern on the same subject. According to him in order to 'perpetuate' the view that the Muslims are aggressive and a threat to society the media primarily focused on al-Qaeda, the Taliban and jihad against the West, and marginal figures such as Abu Hamza al-Masri.

The media is saturated with these types of figures, due in part to its populist approach. It aspires to seize the attention of the masses at any cost. According to some respondents this misrepresentation can occur in another form; the media can introduce someone who is not entitled to represent Muslims. The person could be a non-practicing Muslim or a secular Muslim, or not familiar with Islam at all. S/he may not understand the needs, problems and attitudes of mainstream Muslims. Regardless of these facts just because the person says what people are conditioned to hear, the media allows him/her to speak in the name of Islam or Muslims.

The case of Newsnight

One of the striking examples to this instance was witnessed in the recent cartoon crisis. On 2 February 2006, Newsnight devoted a programme to the cartoons of the Prophet Muhammad (peace be upon him) published by several European newspapers. Their publication outraged many Muslims on account of their abusive and offensive nature. Several guests were present on the programme. They came from different backgrounds. Munira Mirza was introduced as a secular Muslim and academic. She favoured the publication of the cartoons since she believed that in democratic and free countries people should be open any kind of ideas and oppose any kind of censorship. According to her extreme interpretation of freedom - Sardar (2006) names this kind of interpretation of freedom as 'jungle freedom' - she also favoured no censorship of racism or child pornography.
Her views ran against the grain of the majority of Muslims and was subsequently explained by her admission in a BBC Radio 4 programme that she was an atheist.

Some respondents complained that Muslims are given an opportunity only when something negative happened. Therefore, Muslims were always seen on the defensive rather than being allowed to present themselves as proactive citizens.

> Muslims in Britain do not really have a voice; rather, a few select individuals who make inflammatory remarks are given front page news coverage. These people do not in anyway represent the

Muslim community in this country at all, the media are well aware of this and continue to give a voice to those who do not deserve it, regardless of it's consequences to the Muslim Community.

The media is not interested in the plight of the Muslims, instead it seems hell-bent on waging a propaganda war against Islam. Due to the media the words fundamentalist, terrorist and extremist are now synonymous with the words Muslim and Islam.

(Male, 25, West Midlands)

Not much. But if they do, they only show the bits on media which are good (benefit) for them, thereby not allowing the Muslims to say what he actually wants to say. They search for faults in the speech of the Muslims and show only that. In the programme of "the Arabs and Israelis" shown on BBC on Mondays – they do not translate properly. The Palestinian said "I have my Israeli ID card" but it was translated as "I stole an ID card and I forged it"

(Female, 21, London)

They provide little opportunity & that opportunity is often given to people who are unsuitable.

(Male, 23, Nottingham)

Not much opportunity as media is controlled by groups of people who are against Islam.

(Female, 24, London)

Very little, from the wrong people

(Male, 20, Bradford)

Muslims are only given a chance when something negative happens therefore they are not really given a chance.

(Female, 22, London)

However, some respondents blamed the Muslims and their passivity along with the media. They suggested that some positive portrayals could be utilized for the benefit of Muslims:

There is some active opportunity- which I don't think we as Muslims take up very much. I feel that we are also to blame partly because we are not pro-active in "marketing" ourselves. Negative portrayals come in the form of negative news etc. but positive portrayals should be utilized to their maximum benefit. BBC Radio Kent gives me the opportunity to paint a true picture and give my views on subjects.

(Male, 35, Gillingham)

It is up to the people to make their own opportunities by being a bit more active in the media, even if it is just writing a small letter (and make dua to Allah).

(Female, 22, Edinburgh)

According to table 14 there is a correlation between those who believe the media is Islamophobic and 'there is only nominal representation with 'no' (70.2%) and 'no, there is no such representation at all' (65.7%). The table also shows that among those who believe that there is an 'intensive representation in the media', there is a greater degree of negative feelings (Islamophobic (40.0%) and racist (26.7%)) towards the media.

Table 14:	Representation and Perception of Media					
	I have no idea	Islamophobic	Racist	Fair representation of Muslims	Overtly fair representation but covertly destructive	TOTAL
I have no idea	43 51.2%	23 27.4%	8 9.5%	5 6.0%	5 6.0%	84 100.0%
Yes, over representation	2 25.0%	2 25.0%	2 25.0%	1 12.5%	1 12.5%	8 100.0%
Yes, extensive representation	1 6.7%	6 40.0%	4 26.7%	3 20.0%	1 6.7%	15 100.0%
Yes, sufficient representation	5 6.0%	31 37.3%	28 33.7%	14 16.9%	5 6.0%	83 100.0%
No, there is no such representation at all	23 6.3%	241 65.7%	58 10.2%	14 2.5%	78 13.7%	568 100.0%
It is only nominal representation with no.	19 3.3%	399 70.2%	58 10.2%	14 2.5%	78 13.7%	568 100.0%
Total	93 8.3%	702 62.4%	175 15.6%	45 4.0%	110 9.8%	1125 100.0%

MUSLIM EXPECTATIONS FROM THE MEDIA

JUST AND RELIABLE REPRESENTATION

Most of the respondents expect the media to be fair and objective towards Muslims. They want to see reliable reporters who are well versed with the Islamic belief system and cultures or Muslim reporters who can understand their subjects.

I expect them to represent Muslims fairly, which I don't believe is being done. A report published on the BBC news website revealed that due to media representation, an overwhelming amount of people believed that Israel was being occupied by Palestine . This example alone illustrates and summarises the problem.

> To report upon Islam and Muslims through well trusted people or through Muslims themselves. To be uncontrolled by any party or people or even any school of thought.
> (Male, 20, Nottingham)

> I don't expect much since I know who controls the media in the west. However, I hope that some objectivity is portrayed in the programmes and the truth about the essence of Islam must be expressed without any prejudice.
> (Male, 43, Edinburgh)

> Give them more of a chance to voice their opinions. More neutral reporting needed.
> (Female, 27, London

A BALANCED APPROACH

Moreover, respondents suggested that the media should be balanced in its approach and try to understand what is going on in the minds of the Muslim population and convey it as it is. Some even argued that they should be careful with the vocabulary that they use in or order to avoid any negative perception.

> A balanced approach with due consideration to respected viewpoints is essential.
> (Male, 33, Batley)

> Every story has two sides to it. It would be nice of the media to show all the different points of view and not just pick on the controversial ones.
> (Female, 22, Edinburgh)

> That they give them a fair opportunity to voice their side of the story and at least TRY to remain neutral about what's going on. Even some of the vocabulary that is used is inciting hatred in the hearts of those watching against Muslims.
> (Female, 23, London)

COVERAGE REGARDING OTHER ASPECTS OF ISLAM

Other respondents suggested that instead of bringing up political issues, other aspects of Islam should be covered by the media i.e. art, culture, science and civilization.

> Really, a more balanced representation is needed to reflect the true sentiments of the Muslim community. Other positive aspects of Islam should be covered such as arts, culture, science and Islamic civilization.
> (Male, 20, London)

GIVING MORE OPPORTUNITIES TO MUSLIMS IN THE MEDIA

Some suggested that Muslims should be given more opportunities in the media so they could represent themselves better.

> I would hope to see more opportunity for Muslims to voice their opinions relating to Muslim issues.
> (Female, 21, Batley)

> I think they need to do more researchers out there and get more Muslims involved in the media ………..
> (Female, 30, Oldham)

LEGAL PROTECTION

Respondents suggested that the government should take steps to protect Muslims from biased coverage. This might be in the form of legislation which prevents the media insulting Islam and Muslims and to prosecuting people who incite hatred against Islam. As Jews and Sikhs have full protection against religious discrimination in Britain on the grounds that they are considered a race and are therefore covered by anti-racism legislation a similar law could be enacted for Muslims and other faith based communities in order to heal their heavily bruised trust. The law would allow the authorities to deal appropriately with people like the BNP chief Nick Griffin who openly called Islam a "vicious wicked religion."

> Although, bias will inevitably exist, I feel that there should be some sort of legislation or standards, to ensure the levels of negative portrayals of Muslims, and especially Islam, are not at the outstanding levels they are today.
> (Male, 18, London)

It seems that the general perception of the media within the Muslim community is extremely negative. Muslims seem to be very disappointed with the negative media coverage of Muslims, which portrays Muslims as terrorist, backward, misogynistic, uncivilized and violent people. The vast majority of respondents believe that the negative portrayal of Muslims by the media is a part of a political agenda that serves the interest of the political elite. The findings also suggest that there is great dismay and outrage within the Muslim community as a reaction to what they believe is the media onslaught on Muslims. These findings seriously damage the image of British media which is meant to be one of the main pillars of the Western civilization supposedly promoting justice, liberty and equality of all human kind.

REMARKS FROM COMMUNITY FIGURES, ACADEMICS AND PRACTITIONERS

IHRC asked community actvivists, researchers, practitioners and activists for their thoughts on the issues raised.

NASFIM HAQUE,
BBC WALES

I think the media is a main player in creating a public perception, I don't know if there is demonisation across the board but certainly clear categorisation by using words which suit the liberal agenda like "extreme" or "moderate" where the latter are only acceptable and 'integrated' and certainly mainstream media is responsible for or comfortable with caricaturing Muslims as bearded or head covering and where all the women have forced marriages. There is certainly a huge lack of understanding of subtleties and of cultures and of course in a so called secular society a measuring of the progressiveness of Islam through a western prism. So in that respect the media has created false images, often though sadly helped by members of the Muslim community (many are scared to rock the boat and are first generation Muslims) who apologise or who help perpetuate myths and also happy to sell Islam by a western yard stick.

I think though the mainstream media TV, press and radio shouldn't be so scared of the subject and Muslims also should learn to present it more savvily and with wit and humour use the western forms of presentation to really get Islam across, rather than being so worthy and alienating.

Although we have to bear in mind that the British Media ultimately is controlled and editorially held by people who have a very different agenda to the one of promoting a religion like Islam positively, and it is too easy to think that by getting Muslims at the top we can change this- the reality is, that for one reason or another many practising Muslims will never get to the top of the media tree so they can never influence policy in the media overall.

Muslims as a community need to present a more coherent united front to the media. Muslims also have to get their arguments clear amongst themselves and need to be savvy and articulate and friendly when talking to the media, we also need clear leadership as a community overall and not have old fuddy duddy Asian men represent us. Of course, it helps having more Muslims practising and breaking in to the media, and InshAllah that's happening, but more mainstream rather than ghettoised media, so there is a learning process and process of dialogue, and more non Muslims become used to it.

Muslims should also be weary of being pitted against another Muslim on mainstream media outlets i.e. showing us to be a fragmented community so not to actually appear on shows where they might be put against other members of the Muslim community in an argument, so really to scrutinise any media requests.

Should normalise Muslims on screen and encourage deeper debate no matter how scary and to embrace Muslims from all groups rather than silencing them. The media should also look for positive stories rather than negative, sensational ones. The media also should demonise bigotry of any kind and create an atmosphere where such intolerance is unacceptable and government has a role in this.

I think the government are becoming more right wing, arguably using paranoia as a way to control the masses, I expect this to sadly get worse. I think the media may follow suit if under pressure to keep audiences, as I genuinely believe Islam is the biggest subject on policy makers' minds in terms of global stability and interests. I don't think media portrayal will alter vastly, Muslims can only change this by offering and presenting a more positive, united front and confronting problems in our own community and bettering ourselves so there are no bad stories to report

ARUN KUNDNANI,
DEPUTY EDITOR OF THE JOURNAL RACE & CLASS.

I would identify four confusions in the prevailing discourse about British Muslims in the media. These four confusions reflect and reinforce Islamophobia in British society.

i) There is confusion and deliberate blurring of the distinctions between Islam itself, the diverse and varied political movements that draw on Islam for their ideology, armed groups which adopt an Islamist ideology in fighting for self-determination and the 'global terrorism' that is associated with al-Qa'ida. The implication is that there is a slippery slope from the first of these to the last.

ii) There is confusion between discussions of multiculturalism in Britain and the question of Muslims in Britain. The issue of multiculturalism in Britain is a question that affects all communities and is a general discussion about how different groups can pursue their own cultures within a single society. Yet the subtext to all the heated debate about multiculturalism at present is that it is exclusively Muslims who present a challenge to 'British core values' and, in doing so, create the problem of diversity.

iii) There is confusion between issues of diversity and immigration with regard to Muslims. When Muslims are presented as challenging Britain's 'core values' and calling into question the possibility of a diverse society, the question of their right to be resident in Britain is invoked. Numerous commentators have said, 'if Muslims don't accept this country's values, then get out'. Yet diversity is a question of citizenship not immigration. Most Muslims are not foreigners and most foreigners are not Muslims.

iv) There is a confusion of issues of faith with issues of culture or with issues of social exclusion. Thus, Islam gets blamed for the social exclusion of British Pakistanis and Bangladeshis, whereas in fact this is the result of racial discrimination and cultural rather than religious factors.

Similarly, practices such as forced marriage are seen as being an aspect of Islam rather than being seen as a cultural practice that is common to most traditional societies.

In these four ways, Islam becomes construed as a threat to British security and identity, whether on the military, terrorist, demographic or cultural level. This discourse reaches its apotheosis in the influential writings of Niall Ferguson, Rod Liddle and Melanie Phillips but it is reflected generally across the newspapers in both news and commentary sections, in broadcast media, particularly political discussion programmes, in internet and radio phone-in discussions and in popular fiction.

My recommendations to counter this are:

i) Organisations that work on issues of anti-racism, community cohesion, faith relations and human rights need to be prepared to take a much stronger stand in speaking out against these ways of thinking and publicly denounce those who adopt such a discourse, even if, as is increasingly the case, those who do so are speaking from a position of sound 'liberal' or 'left-wing' credentials.

ii) There ought to be stronger relationships between Muslim organisations in Britain and groups that have campaigned against racism and prejudice in the media. Although such alliances will present challenges to both parties, they are a pre-requisite to bringing about change.

iii) The government needs to end its strategy of denial about the underlying causes of last year's terrorist attacks and acknowledge that many people in British society feel anger and despair about the government's imperialist project in Iraq and Afghanistan. Such anger does not emanate from 'Muslim fanaticism' but from legitimate grievances shared by many non-Muslims. As long as the government continues its politics of denial, it will continue to give the imprimatur of the state to all kinds of Islamophobic ideas.

DR ANTHONY MCROY,

LECTURER IN ISLAMICS, EVANGELICAL THEOLOGICAL COLLEGE OF WALES, AUTHOR OF FROM RUSHDIE TO JULY 7, 2005: THE RADICALISATION OF ISLAM IN BRITAIN.

The media has helped to demonise Muslims through a mixture of ignorance and malice. The most obvious example of ignorance is jihad; no media pieces ever explained the difference between *offensive* and *defensive* jihad, the bases for, and conditions attached to both. This demonises Muslims since it convinces the public that jihad has no other motive than conquest. Further, the media never distinguish the jihads of HAMAS and Hezbollah on the one hand, and Al-Qaida on the other. Secondly, the media rarely distinguishes between Islamists such as Ghannouchi and Tamimi, who insist that democracy is compatible with Islam, and individuals such as Zawahiri who oppose this.

The latter point is linked to the undue attention fringe elements receive and their effective portrayal as representative Muslims. It is also connected to the equally undue attention given to hostile commentators with a fixed political agenda, especially on foreign policy. An example is the way former Israeli Premier Barak was included in a group of 'experts' on a BBC programme after 9/11.

The urgent need is for the media to become educated in these areas. There should also be more attention given to the British-born generation, since their involvement makes Muslims appear less 'foreign'. A positive step would be for practising Muslims wearing Hijab/beard to be recruited as newsreaders and presenters. This would help reduce Islamophobia. However, it must be recognised that the media loves a good scandal, and that Islamophobia aids government foreign policy, so any expectations of change should be limited.

ISMAIL ADAM PATEL,
FRIENDS OF AL AQSA

Today's media with its razzle and dazzle, instant information, phenomenal graphics and camera tricks has occupied a position in the centre of our social culture and in particular the news media plays the most dominant role in shaping our emotions and thoughts of the outside world.

However, the reality of images we see or information we receive is not all it is made up to be. Because behind every event that is being portrayed there is a storyteller, behind whom are editors and a band of bureaucrats ensuring the story is told according to their perception, they have an agenda that is not necessarily concurrent with our beliefs nor is it the 'truth'.

In other words the media, which has become our tool for information has its own agenda and the media, which we so heavily rely upon for our daily diet of news is neither in our control nor of our making. However it has the potential to shape our ideas, our thoughts as well as our view of the world.

The media in general but TV in particular has been the most derogatory, from the Muslims point of view. In most recent movies, the Arabs, which are synonymous with Muslims are shown as bloodthirsty savages, obstacles to progress, predators on peaceful 'West', and are portrayed as enemy "hostiles" of the U.S. and the West.

The West is portrayed as a freedom-loving nation which is forced to bring the savages of the Arab lands into control. This idea of us and them goes towards justifying the torture, imprisonment and even murder and everything else upon the 'other' barbarians as this is portrayed and perceived to be carried out for their benefit.

Many Muslims who have become the casual absorbers of this type of propaganda become disillusioned with their faith. Many Muslims internalise these media images, leading to a self-loathing, and a rejection of their own history and their own past.

This is called "Cultural imperialism" – where one culture ('First World') exports cultural products to another society (usually in the 'Third' or 'Fourth' world) with the goal of a) eliminating native cultural and b) replacing them with "alien" representations which in turn are supposed to c) transform the culture so that it loses its autonomy and becomes 'assimilated' into the global capitalist world-system.

EMDAD RAHMAN,
NEWS EDITOR BANGLA MIRROR ENGLISH WEEKLY
ENGLISH EDITOR EURO BANGLA NATIONAL BILINGUAL
WEEKLY, EDITORIAL ASSISTANT THE LONDON MUSLIM

1: Attitudes towards British Muslims; A survey commissioned by the Islamic Society of Britain found that out of approximately 2000 people, 66% said that the TV and newspapers were the biggest source of their information about Britain's Muslim community.

The media has always been seen as having been at the forefront of the denigration of Muslims.

In the present light of day, there is no religion more misconstrued and misapprehended than Islam. Many say that this current onslaught has been in operation since the collapse of communism, thus enabling the media juggernaut to install Islam as the latest opponent to global peace and wellbeing.

The Runnymede Trust says that Britain has become "an institutionally Islamophobic" society in which Muslims are demonised.

This is not just limited to Britain. In his book "Imaginary Islam: The media's construction of Islamophobia in France", political commentator Thomas Deltombe described certain congruence in the way Islam is perceived by the French media and by ultra-conservative Muslims.

Elizabeth Poole, a lecturer in Media and Cultural Studies at the School of Humanities and Social Science, Staffordshire University carried out a three year study during the 90's in which she discovered that media topics were framed, often giving rise to the expression of a few central defining themes: that Muslims are a threat to security in the UK due to their involvement in illicit activities; that Muslims are a threat to British mainstream values and thus provoke integrative concerns; that there are inherent cultural differences between Muslims and the host community which create tensions in interpersonal relations; that Muslims are increasingly making their presence felt in the public sphere.

When Chechens fight back, this is labelled Islamic terrorism. If we employ the same reasoning then the carnage caused by Russian forces engaged in widespread killing, arson, rape and looting in incidents such as at Grozny and Chernokozova, dubbed the "factory of death" should be labelled as Russian terror campaigns. However this is not the case and countless examples such as this only serve to create further barriers.

2: It is felt that all Muslims should pay for gross actions that they do not agree with. Islam is a religion of peace. If the notion that all Muslims are terrorists were true then countries like the UK would really be faced with a problem. George Bernard Shaw once said that "If any religion had the chance of ruling over England, nay Europe within the next hundred years, it could be Islam." The demonisation of Muslims is leading non Muslims to research the tenets of this great religion thus many are converting to Islam.

I agree that it is necessary to recommend strategies to reduce the malicious slandering of Muslims by increasing positive public awareness about them, their cultures and their religions, by improving official responses to discrimination and by enhancing the appreciation among all communities of the very positive benefits of cultural diversity.

3: The media instead of being one of the primary architects of Islamophobia could be active in confronting it. Whilst the idea of a free media in Britain must always be defended, the Department of Culture, Media & Sport (DCMS) and individual media and popular culture industries and agencies can play an important role in developing and influencing the national public culture away from Islamophobia, as they have done in the case of other forms of prejudices.

4: The Home Office report into the Bradford riots suggested there that immigrants should be made to swear an oath of allegiance to Britain. This asks questions of the Muslim understanding of multiculturalism and if it is the same as the British government's. I agree with Iqbal Sacranie when he said that you change the society by ensuring that there is a clear and honest feeling prevailing on the ground, that everyone is part of the community. You do that by ensuring that opportunities are offered equally to all sections of what makes up the British public.

Statistics indicate that Bangladeshis and Pakistanis are bottom of the table in terms of achievers, in terms of education, housing and social state of affairs. This can only come out by educating, by providing information through media, through government departments, police authorities and others, for them to have a better understanding of the community and vice versa. It's a two-way process.

YVONNE RIDLEY,
JOURNALIST, AUTHOR AND POLITICAL EDITOR OF ISLAM CHANNELL

The Western media has been extremely influential in the demonisation process of Muslim communities around the world to such an extent that some people automatically think of terrorism when they see a Hijab or a beard.

For instance journalists are 100 times more likely to associate Islam with terrorism than all other faiths combined. This particular fact emerged recently after a word search study was carried out on articles written in American newspapers about Islam over the last 10 years. Part of this is due to ignorance from journalists but much of it is down to an institutional Islamophobic streak running through western newsrooms. There is also evidence of government approval and encouragement.

The European Union is also aware of these factors and is hoping new guidelines using a more restrained language and phraseology to discuss so-called radicalism may have an impact. For instance they want to avoid phrases like 'Islamic terrorism' when discussing terrorism which may be carried out in the name of Islam.

Islamist, fundamentalists and jihadists are written about in authoritative tones by some journalists who clearly have no idea of their true meaning. This is often blindingly obvious to Muslim readers and those coming from a point of knowledge, but to the average reader the message is clear ... terrorism is inextricably linked to the world's 2.2 billion Muslims. In reality 99.9 per cent of those Muslims will never carry out an act of terrorism, fund terrorism, know a terrorist let alone use Islam to justify an act of terrorism. The percentage of those Muslims who will become or are victims of state terrorism are much reduced, something the reader may want to ponder. The reality is that the largest number of so-called suicide bombers come from Sri Lanka's Tamil Tigers, a Marxist- Leninist group whose members are mainly of the Hindu faith.

Should I, as a woman, fear all men because all rapists are men?

Journalists are deliberately associating Islam with terrorism. I cannot believe my colleagues are collectively so stupid... we need to find out why they are doing this and what is the real motive and agenda.

CONCLUDING REMARKS: THE BIG LIE AND DEMONIZED REPRESENTATION

Disassociating representation from the idea that it somehow holds the essence of truth even in its most fictionalised forms, is not a new concept, and some form of scepticism regarding representation is a healthy development. Serious arguments in the philosophy of art and media regarding the negativity of particularly visual culture in Western thought, originated in the philosophy of Plato. Plato believed that the objects encountered in everyday life, including people, are simply bad copies of the perfect idea of those objects. He compared this reproduction as being like the shadows cast by a fire on a cave wall-you can see who or what cast the shadow but the image is inevitably distorted from the original's appearance. In other words, everything we see in the real world is already a copy. For an artist to make a representation of what is seen would be to make a copy of a copy, increasing the chance of distortion (Plato, 1991: 286 – cited in Mirzoeff, 1999:9). A more conscious understanding on the part of representers and a confidence on the part of the audience to engage and interrogate can eliminate the demonisation that results from ongoing structural causes and expose where it is consciously promoted, as false.

With the proliferation of new, alternative and independent media, and growing scepticism about mainstream media including literature, cinema and particularly news media, there can now come a point where mainstream forms of representation become exposed in the popular psyche as the "Big Lie". At this stage, the audience will not trust anything produced by the established 'media'. Such an environment can adversely affect 'national trust', national solidarity and at the end it can detrimentally affect peace and stability in society.

The findings from this work suggest that Muslims at least have decoded very anti-Muslim practices within the media that, if understood and articulated wider, could expose critical faults within cultural discourse that indict the mainstream cultural practice. The UK has seen a sea change in its reporting and its cultural activity to (try to) overcome inherent racism as well as anti-Semitic and even anti-Catholic prejudice and bias towards non-conformists. The portrayal of sexuality has also benefited from the operation of normative considerations at structural levels within cultural institutions from TV and radio companies to universities and art galleries. However just as many would argue that the struggle with regard to racism is far from won, anti-Muslim prejudice – the specificity of Islamophobic representation – has become a recognisable theme in representation that has yet to result in ethical re-evaluation at any serious level.

From a human rights perspective this is disappointing and potentially disastrous. Demonized representation is one of the deepest and most effective anti-human rights practices, as it has the potential not just to libel or demonize a particular person, but it can demonize all members of the represented community e.g. all Muslims or all British Muslims. The potential for societal discord as a result is clear and as the research of this series shows, is in part understood to be having serious repercussions on the everyday lives of minorities, particularly Muslim minorities in the UK.

If, however, demonised representation can be decoded and dealt with institutionally, then a chaotic, even anarchic response to the 'Big Lie' at a societal level can be avoided. To do so, steps need to be taken to ensure that the decoding of prejudice, not simply against Muslims - although this is the focus of this research - happens because the reality of the demonised minority is revealed through media structures. If a contradictional picture between a minority's reality and the representation of it happens through a wholesale disillusionment with established media and culture, the societal impacts are uncertain. When representation is related to a collective identity such as religious community, ethnic group or a particular nation, then the tendency of language is to be universal. In this sense 'one' becomes equal to all and 'all become equal to one'. Here, if it is understood through a process of cultural decoding that firstly that equation was incorrect and 'one was not equal to all' and second that reality itself was not rightly represented, the "Big Lie" becomes obvious for many or all. In this step, reverse representation starts and the whole discourse of representation becomes questioned by society. A 'good and great America' produced by Hollywood as well as a bad enemy of say 'Japan and China' or 'Islam and Muslim' represented in the media can only be workable until the reality is understood by the majority.

If that contradictional picture is exposed as part of a learning curve that takes mainstream society and media on a journey of societal cohesion through a process of interrogating culturally defined givens, then there is hope for the development of a truly engaged citizenship that needs and uses the media to negotiate its existence.

RECOMMENDATIONS

This volume, more than others, requires recommendations that can be implemented by both government and other relevant institutions. Media regulation is a contentious subject and the interests of free speech require sensitivity. However, as previous volumes in this series have shown, hate speech and anti-Muslim racism, perceived and often defined as Islamophobia require action that necessarily curtails free speech to the minimum extent required to ensure that other human rights are protected and effected. Three strands of action need to be worked on: tackling structural / institutionalized Islamophobia; dealing with problematic content; and facilitating understanding of Muslim standpoint(s) within the media.

TACKLING INSTITUTIONAL ISLAMOPHOBIA
MONITORING REPRESENTATION OF MUSLIMS

Repeatedly, respondents in this research (across the series) point to misrepresentation of Muslims in art, literature, TV fiction, news and factual programming, cinema etc. as not only offensive and upsetting but as having social impact on their lives. Particularly but not solely, television news and television broadcasters need to monitor their output and how Muslims are represented within that. This needs to look at not only the type of very specific issues of bias examined by the BBC regarding the Palestinian / Israeli conflict, but other news stories, positive representation versus negative representation in the news, involvement of Muslims in storylines of drama and other fictional programmes, and quality of such representation. Notable complaints include the perpetual portrayal of Muslims in dramas as problematic, terrorists, violent, misogynistic etc, and necessarily so as defined by their religion. By perpetuating such stereotypes, the cycle of vilification remains unbroken. As drama often follows news, many long running series are currently weaving terrorist criminality involving Muslims into their plots. Other recurring storylines involve forced marriage. There are few if any notable fictional characters who are incidentally (religiously) Muslim or whose religiosity is a positive factor in a storyline.

Monitoring Muslim representation – if done in good faith and not simply as a sop to criticism, helps to create better drama, better standards of reporting and has a knock on effect on how Muslim minorities are viewed by non-Muslims, and also on how Muslims view the media.

Whilst the initial onus of this must be on broadcasters and those responsible for media representation of Muslims, government needs to be involved in this process, commissioning studies if necessary or facilitating the requisite debate around alienation and the impact of media on the process, in the hope that this will generate more than just a superficial self-analysis by media producers.

TACKLING OVERT VILIFICATION AND DEMONISATION OF MUSLIMS

Where vilification of Muslims and Islam is overt and arguably deliberate, effective recourse must be made available to those offended to (i) complain about offending work; (ii) to achieve some form of recompense, either by way of apology, correction or right of reply. Whilst individuals can make use of existing press and broadcasting codes to get some recourse, more generalised demonisation, be it in the print media, in a fictional drama or TV / radio news, cannot easily be criticised. Issues to do with more powers for watchdogs will be discussed below, however government needs to find ways of penalizing overt vilification and demonisation. Inevitably this includes incorporating discrimination against religious minorities into various laws to ensure that hate speech covers speech against Muslims, and that race relations laws apply equally to all religious communities. Arguments that free speech will be curtailed by such actions are anomalous as race relations laws already exists that curtail free speech when ethnic minorities are discussed and indeed some religious communities.

CULTURAL CHANGE IN THE ATTITUDE OF BRITISH POLITICIANS

It is crucial to have a cultural change in the way the politicians utilize the media in the way they deal with the minorities. Due to disparity of access to the media political comments cannot be countered and debated in a way that includes minority groups. As such the media becomes a destructive force and a blunt instrument to force minorities into certain positions, thus, creating demonization between the majority and the minorities.

DEALING WITH PROBLEMATIC CONTENT
CREATING EFFECTIVE WATCHDOGS

As discussed above, current watchdogs afford little scope for people to complain about generalised prejudice in the media. Respondents in this research stated time and again that they had given up complaining about misrepresentation as nothing was done. Watchdogs need to be able to take or recommend real punitive action against media institutions who deliberately or negligently allow prejudicial representation. This requires government to enact relevant legislation to create watchdogs "with teeth".

The existence of such powers will prevent issues getting to this stage, and require media institutions to onerously self-regulate. Complaining to media institutions currently does not even elicit a response. This creates further disillusionment amongst Muslims in mainstream institutions and also feeds irresponsible production.

CREATING STRUCTURES OF ACCOUNTABILITY FOR THE POLITICAL USE OF MEDIA.

In addition, including provisions for accountability in the ministerial and parliamentary codes of conduct could be an effective way of dealing with the acts of politicians which might have those effects.

REQUIRING BALANCE

Whilst broadcasting regulatory codes state that balance is required, the press in particular has much room to be partisan. Whilst left and right wing views are easily discernable to a mainstream audience when talking about the health service, or environmental policy, bias against Muslims is not easily recognisable and politicised agendas regarding say e.g. support for international resistance groups, or new legislation regarding hate speech, are not easily understood to be partisan expressions linked to other political agendas. As a result, ideas that often reflect a journalist or commentator's own views and bias are understood to be representations of objective fact. Again this issue has relevance not just for Muslim minorities, but minorities per se, and the requirement of balance needs to be looked at with specific regard to muted minority voices.

TAKING ACTION AGAINST WORST OFFENDERS

Despite the best efforts of institutions to make effective change, persistent and problematic demonisation persists. Certain columnists now make a living out of anti-Muslim diatribes often dressed up as a professional interest in either terrorism, homeland security, Middle East affairs, or social cohesion and race relations. The relevance of non-discriminatory anti-discrimination legislation pertains here, as it would require the use of such tests that editors and producers apply when assessing content that affects e.g. Jewish and Sikh communities who are protected under race relations law, and applying such tests to the representation of Muslims and other religious minorities. These tests should not prevent effective critique of religion or religious minorities. However as no effective case or challenge has been made by either right or left wing commentators that such a curtailment happens under existing race laws, a new assessment needs to be made across the board.

ACCOUNTABILITY

Ultimately there has to be more accountability for the demonisation and vilification of minorities in the media. Clearly where problems arise in cinema, censors need more power to be able to curtail or even decline certification of objectionable material. Filmmakers cannot be exempt from non-discrimination norms, by virtue of being an 'artist'. TV News editors cannot repeatedly allow misreporting under the excuse of time constraints. Self-regulation needs to be coupled with effective forms of accountability which ultimately only government can set. At a time when government is intent on curtailing free speech under the guise of anti-terrorism laws, it cannot claim the defence of free speech in this or any other case. Either the impact of all speech is assessed or none. Anything less simply confirms that Britain today is replete with and multiplying old and new hierarchies that not only posit (Muslim) minorities at the very bottom, but demonise them as incapable of being anywhere else.

UNDERSTANDING MUSLIM STANDPOINT(S)

(I) CONTEXTUALISING REPORTING OF ISLAM

Whilst much diversity of opinion exists within Islam, there is still an issue of lack of context pertaining to the reporting of Islam specifically. Controversial ideas – understood as either 'liberal' or 'extremist' - are often portrayed as mainstream and acceptable or mainstream and inflexible, respectively. Neither are the multiple perspectives afforded by Muslim diversity heard, but even basic and uncontroversial aspects of Islam are portrayed in negative and uncontexualised ways. Thus 'arranged' marriages are portrayed as forced marriages rather than marriages by introduction and are assumed to be the norm. Where attempts are made to research issues, again very specific research is often used to generalise about all Muslims of whatever ethnicity, upbringing, school of thought etc. Whilst there are time constraints and technical difficulties involved, particularly in news reporting, in providing more context, the example of the appointment of a senior correspondent to provide context on the Palestinian / Israeli conflict is a good way of showing improved, though still imperfect, practice. Given the prevalence of Islam related stories, such moves are a step in the right direction.

(II) WIDE AND EFFECTIVE CONSULTATION

The government and media should consult with scholars that are qualified to give rulings and statements, and state which scholars they have consulted. Some Hollywood productions, notably the 1999 movie *Three Kings* have done so. Providing names again requires that consultants be more professional and less parochial in their outlook, providing balanced as well as specialised advice. It also enables those with questions about the validity of portrayals or discussions about Muslims to provide effective critiques. This research has shown time and again that Muslims welcome debate and discussion about their beliefs and values – what they complain about is that they are unable to articulate their viewpoints and reciprocate critique on a level playing field. Further, the failure of media institutions to try and understand Muslim views, is another way of muting (an) already largely silenced community/ies. Where dramas have sought to seek out the views of those they portray e.g. Channel 4's film *Yasmin* and the film *Three Kings*, even where substantial issue is taken with parts of that representation both films have generally been respected by Muslims as honest attempts to engage with them.

As with other volumes in this series, consultation with Muslims is not simply about consulting on 'Muslim' issues. Muslims are also media consumers and in so far as media – from high art to local radio news – speaks to an audience, Muslims must be understood to form part of that audience. If they or any other group are missing, media producers need to question why that is, and if, as in the case of the mass media, what implications this has on its credibility.

The recommendations listed above are not exhaustive or indeed particularly concrete. However they do point to issues raised by respondents that require media providers – if they aspire to democratic and human rights values – to rethink how they work and what they provide.

BIBLIOGRAPHY

Abbas, T. (2000) 'Images of Islam', *Index on Censorship*, Vol. 29 (5), (September/October 2000), pp. 64-68.

Abbas, T. (ed) (2005) *Muslim Britain: Communities under Pressure*, London: Zed.

Abdelmoteleb, M. (2005) *Robin Hood and the Muslim Merry Man,* Islam Online www.islamonline.net (Accessed 28 August 2006).

Ahmed, A. F. (1992) *Post Modernism and Islam: Predicament and Promise*, New York, Routledge.

Allen, C. & Nielsen, J. (2002) 'Summary Report on Islamophobia' in the EU after 11 September 2001, Vienna: European Monitoring Centre on Racism and Xenophobia.

Allen, C. (2005) 'From Race to Religion. The New Face of Discrimination' in Abbas, T, *Muslim Britain* pp 49-65. London: Zed.

Al-Shaykh, H. (1993) *Women of Sand & Myrrh,* United Kingdom: Quartet Books.

Ameli, S. R. & Merali, A. (2004a) *Dual Citizenship: British, Islamic or Both? Obligation, Recognition, Respect and Belonging,* London: Islamic Human Rights Commission.

Ameli, S. R., Elahi, M. & Merali, A. (2004b) *Social Discrimination: Across the Muslim Divide,* London: Islamic Human Rights Commission.

Ameli, S. R., Azam, A. & Merali, (2005) *Secular or Islamic: What Scholls do British Muslims want for their children?,* London: Islamic Human Rights Commission.

Ameli, S. R., & Merali, A. (2006a) *Hijab Meaning, Identity, Otherization and Politics: British Muslim Women*, London: Islamic Human Rights Commission.

Ameli, S. R., Faridi, B., Lindahl, K. & Merali, A. (2006b) *Law and British Muslims: Domination of the Majority or Process of the Balance?,* London: Islamic Human Rights Commission.

Andrew, J. D. (1984) *Concepts in film theory.* Oxford: Oxford University Press.

Ansari, K. H. (2002) *Muslims in Britain*, Minority Rights Group International.

Ansari, K. H. (2004) *The Infidel Within: The History of Muslims in Britain 1800 to the present,* C.Hurst & Co Publishers.

Ansari, K. H. (2005) London Terrorist Attacks: The Impact of 7/7 on British Muslims, (ARI) http://www.realinstitutoelcano.org/analisis/780.asp

Arnold, M. (1865) *Essays in Criticism First Series,* London: MacMillan.

Ashcroft, B. & P. Ahluwalia. (1999) *Edward Said: The Paradox of Identity*, London: Routledge.

Baer, J. (1998) *Muted Group Theory by Chris Kramarae*, Human Communication Theory, Colorado: University of Colorado.

BBC, (2004) Mid-East coverage baffles Britons, (http://news.bbc.co.uk/1/hi/world/middle_east/3829967.stm - Accessed June 2006)

Bignell, J. (2004) *An Introduction to Television Studies,* London: Routledge.

Bronte, C. (1991) *Jane Eyre*, Oxford: Oxford University Press.

Bunglawala, I. (2002) 'British Muslims and the Media', in *The Quest for Sanity: Reflections on September 11 and the Aftermath,* London: MCB. pp 43-52.

Campbell, C. P. (1995) *Race, Myth and the News,* California: Sage.

Childs, P. and P. Williams, (1997) *An Introduction to Post- Colonial Theory* Essex: Prentice Hall.

Chomsky, N. (1993) *'Media Control',* Alternative Press Review*:* Fall 1993

Christison, K. (2001) (2nd edition) Perceptions Of Palestine, London: University of California Press.

Clavell, J. (1996) *Escape,* London: Coronet Books.

Conrad, J. (1992) *Heart of the Darkness and Other Tales,* Oxford: Oxford University Press.

Conte, W. (2001) *British Media Portrayals of Muslims. In the Wake of the September 11 Attacks.* http://web.mit.edu/cms/reconstructions/communications/ukmuslims.html

Cottle, S. (ed) (2000) *Ethnic Minorities and the Media: Changing Cultural Boundaries,* Buckingham: Oxford University Press.

Daniel, N. (1960) *Islam and the West: The Making of an Image,* Edinburgh: University Press.

Elmasry, M.I. (2002) *Anti-Islam in the Canadian Media Report*, Canada: the Canadian Islamic Congress.

Fielding, H. (1999) *Bridget Jones' Diary*, London: Penguin.

Fielding, H. (2001) *Bridget Jones' Diary: Edge of Reason*, London: Penguin.

Fregoso, R. L. (1993) 'The Representation of Cultural Identity in "Zoot Suit"' (1981), *Theory and Society*, Vol. 22(5), pp. 659-674.

Gandhi, L. (1998) *Postcolonial Theory: a critical Introduction*, Edinburgh: Edinburgh University Press.

Goodwin, A & Whannel, G. (1995) *Understanding Television.* London: Routledge.

Graber, D. (2nd ed) (1988) *Processing the News: How People Tame the Information Tide*, New York: Longman.

Gurevitch, M., Bennett, T., Curran, J. &Woollacott, J. (1995) *Culture, Commerce, Society and The Media*, London: Routledge.

Hall, S. (1992) 'The West and the Rest', in Hall, S. and Gieben, B. (eds) *Formations of Modernity*, Cambridge, Polity Press/The Open University.

Hall, S. (1975) *TV as a Medium and its Relation to Culture*, CCCS, Birmingham: University of Birmingham.

Hall, S. (1993) 'The Whites of their Eyes: Racist Ideologies in the Media', in Alvarado, M. & Thompson, J, (eds), *The Media Reader*, London: BFI.

Hall, S. (1997) *Representation: Cultural Representations and Signifying Practices*, London: Sage.

Henzell-Thomas, J. (2001) *The Language of Islamophobia*, Paper presented at the 'Exploring Islamophobia' Conference, University of Westminster, 29 September 2001.

Hewitt, I. (July 2006), 'Our Upside Down World', *Q-News*, Issue 367

Hill, D. B. (1981) Political Culture and Female Political Representation, *The Journal of politics*, Vol. 43(1), pp. 159-168.

Hitchens, P. (2003) Will Britain Convert to Islam?, *Mail on Sunday* (http://www.mailonsunday.co.uk/pages/live/articles/columnists/columnists.html?in_article_id=201325&in_page_id=1772&in_author_id= - accessed July 2006)

Huntington, S. P. (1996) *The Clash of Civilizations and the Remaking of World Order*, New York: Simon and Schuster.

IQRA Trust. (1990) *Research on Public Attitudes towards Islam*, Research Report: No.1. IQRA Trust: London.

Kipling, R. (1941) *Kim*, Garden City: Doran.

Kellner, D. (1992). Television the Crisis of Democracy and the Persian Gulf War. In Raboy. M. and Dagenais B. (Eds.), *Media, Crisis and Democracy: Mass Communication and the Disruption of Social Order*. London : Sage.

Lewis, J. (1995) 'Are You Receiving Me?', in Goodwin, A. & Whannel, G., *Understanding Television*, London: Routledge. pp 153-164.

Loomba, A. (1998) *Colonialism/Postcolonialism*, London: Routledge, 1998.

Macfie, A. L. (2002) *Orientalism*, Great Britain: Longman.

Mahmoody, B. & Hoffer, W. (1989) *Not Without My Daughter*, Great Britain: Corgi Books.

Mian, S. T. (1997) '*Islam: Media Representation and Public Perception*', unpublished MSc dissertation, Nottingham Trent University.

Mirzoeff, N. (1999) *An Introduction to Visual Culture*, London and New York, Routledge.

Mistry, R. (1999) *Can Gramsci's theory of hegemony help us to understand the representation of ethnic minorities in Western television and cinema?* www.theory.org.uk/ctr-rol6.htm

Nafisi, A. (2004) *Reading Lolita in Tehran,* New York: Random House.

Naipaul, V.S. (2001) *Among the Believers*. Essex: Picador.

O'Sullivan, T., Hartley, J., Saunders, D., Montgomery, M. & Fiske, J. (1997) *Key Concepts in Communication and Cultural Studies*, Second Edition, London: Routledge.

Phillips, M. (2006) The Country that Hates itself, *Canadian National Post* (http://www.canada.com/nationalpost/news/issuesideas/story.html?id=4e534810-a9d3-40da-8ee8-06abc0b637ed – accessed July 2006)

Philo, G *et al.* (1982) *Bad News* (Vol 3) Really Bad News, GUMG, London: Writers and Readers Publishing Cooperative Society.

Philo, G. & Berry, M. (2004) *Bad News from Israel,* London: Pluto Press.

Poole, E. (2002) *Reporting Islam: Media Representations of British Muslims*. London: I B Tauris.

Plato (1991) *Plato's Republic*, Translated by Allan Bloom, New York: Basic Books.

Raboy, M & Dagenais, B. (1992) *Media, Crisis and Democracy,* London: Sage.

Richardson, J. E. (2001) 'British Muslims in the Broadsheet Press: A Challenge to Cultural Hegemony?', *Journalism Studies*, Vol 2, No 2, 2001, pp 221-242.

Rudnick, L. P., Judith E. Smith & Rachel Lee Rubin, (eds) (2006) *American Identities*, USA: Blackwell Publishing.

Runnymede Trust, (1997) *Islamophobia, A Challenge to us All*, London: The Runnymede Trust.

Runnymede Trust, (2001) *Addressing Prejudice and Islamophobia. Resources, References and Guidance on the Internet*, August 2001, London: Runnymede Trust.

Said, E. (1981) *Orientalism*, London: Routledge and Kegan Paul.

Said, E. W. (1984) *The World, the Text, and the Critic,* London: Faber and Faber.

Said, E. (1994) *Culture and Imperialism*, London: Vintage.

Said, E. (1996) *Covering Islam. How the Media and the Experts Determine How we see the Rest of the World*, New York: Vintage.

Sardar, Z. (1999) *Orientalism,* United Kingdom: Open University Press.

Sardar, Z. (2006). "*A 'freedom' whose home is the jungle*", The Independent (5 February 2006), London.

Sasson, J. (2000) *Desert Royal*, United Kingdom: Bantam Books.

Sasson, J. (1994) *Daughters of Arabia,* United Kingdom: Bantam Books.

Sasson, J. (1993) *Princess*, United Kingdom: Bantam Books.

Satrapi, M. (2000) *Persepolis: The Story of a Childhood,* USA: Pantheon.

Sha'ban, F. (1991) *Islam and Arabs in Early American Thought: The Routes of Orientalism on America,* Durham, N.C. : Acorn Press.

Shaheen, J. (2003) *Reel Bad Arabs: How Hollywood Vilifies a People,* Arris Books.

Spivak, G. C. (1985) 'Three Women's Texts and A Critique of Imperialism' in Henry Louis Gates Jr. ed., *Race, Writing and Difference*, Chicago: University of Chicago Press.

Toynbee, P. (2001) Limp Liberals fail to protect their most profound values, *The Guardian* (http://www.guardian.co.uk/waronterror/story/0,,566722,00.html – accessed July 2006)

Van Dijk, T. (2000) 'New(s) Racism: A Discourse Analytical Approach', in Cottle, S. (ed), *Ethnic Minorities and the Media*, Buckingham: Oxford University Press.

Wahid, A. (July, 2006) 'To care about the ummah is a blessing, not a danger', *Q News*, Issue 367

Whitaker, B. (2002) 'Islam and the British Press After September 11'. (http://www.al-bab.com/media/articles/bw020620.htm (accessed May 2005)

APPENDIX 1:
VISUAL NEWS ANALYSIS (BBC NEWS, NEWSNIGHT, ITV NEWS, CH. 4).

| Investigative Framework (TV News Analysis – BBC News) ||
| *(i) Politics and Security Issues* ||
Category	BBC News - Frequency
Fundamentalist/m	
Terrorism/t	xxxxxx
Extremism/t	xx
Radical	
Militant	
Dissident	
Insurgency	
Terrorist cells	xxxxx
Anti-British	
Anti-Western	
Security	xxx
Threat to national security	
War on terror	
Legislation (anti-terror)	
Global links/dimension	xxx
Foreign policy	
9/11	x
Enemy within/outsider implications	
Immigration Deportation	xx
Asylum seekers	xx
Home Office (visa)	x (JCD)
Names*	xxx (RM) xxxxxx (YHO) xxxx (MSI) xx (JCD)
Al-Qaeda	
Osama bin Laden	
Al-Zawahiri	
Omar Bakri Mohamed	
Anjem Chaudry	
Abu Uzair	
Al-Ghuraba	
Groups [Al-Muhajiroun and HT]	
Tony Blair	x
Bomb/bomber	xxxxxxxxxxxx
Suicide bomb/er	x
Anti-terror (Act)	xxxxxxxxx
Police (investigation)	xxxxxxxxxxxxxxx
IPCC	xx
Stop and search (targeting Muslims)	
Murder/conspiracy to murder	xx
Explosives	x
Iraq	xx
Pakistan	xx
Saudi Arabia	
Afghanistan	
Somalia	x
Eritrea	x
Kenya	
Sudan	
Ethiopia	
East Africa	
Northern Ireland (comparison)	
Paris/Madrid bombings (comparison)	
Interviews – family/public/neighbours etc	xxxxx

Investigative Framework (TV News Analysis – BBC News)	
(ii) Social and Cultural Descriptions	
Category	**BBC News - Frequency**
Loyalty	
Identity	xx
British Muslims	
Gender/women	
Hijab	
Muslim/non-Muslim relations	
Christian/Muslim relations	
Government/Muslim relations	
Conversion	
Islamophobia	
Racism/Racial tensions	
Muslim community	
Segregation/Alienation	
Deprivation/exclusion/inclusion	
Socio-economic status	
Attacks on Muslims/backlash/fear	
Mosques	x
Traditional British values/Assimilation	
Hatred	
Passport/Citizenship	xx

Investigative Framework (TV News Analysis - Newsnight) (iii): Politics and Security Issues	
Category	BBC News - Frequency
Fundamentalist/m	
Terrorism/t	xxxxxxxxxxxxxxxxxxxxxxxxx (IT)
Extremism/t	xxxxxxxxx (IE)
Radical Islamist	xx x
Militant	x (IM)
Dissident	
Insurgency	x
Terrorist cells	xxxxxx
Anti-British	
Anti-West/ern West	x
Security	xxxxxxxxxxx
Threat to national security Terrorist threat	xxxx xx
War on terror	xxxxx
Legislation (anti-terror)	xxxxxx
Global links/dimension	xxx
Foreign policy	xxxxx
9/11	xxx
Enemy within/outsider implications	
Immigration Deportation	x xxxxxx
Asylum seekers	xxx
Home Office (visa)	
Names* xxx (YHO) x (MSI) x (RM) xxx (HO) xx (JCD)	
Al-Qaeda	xxxxxxxxxx
Osama bin Laden	xxxxx
Al-Zawahiri	xxx
Omar Bakri Mohamed	xx
Anjem Chaudry	
Abu Uzair	
Al-Ghuraba	x
Groups [Al-Muhajiroun and HT]	xxx (Al-M) xxx (HT)
Tony Blair	
Bomb/bomber	xxxxxxxxxxxxxx
Suicide bomb/er	xxxxxxxxx
Anti-terror (Act)	xxxxxxx
Police (investigation)	xxxxxxxxxxxx
IPCC	x
Stop and search (targeting Muslims)	xxxxx
Murder/conspiracy to murder	xx
Explosives	
Iraq	
Pakistan	xxx
Saudi Arabia	
Afghanistan	x
Somalia	
Eritrea	
Kenya	
Sudan	
Ethiopia	
East Africa	
Northern Ireland (comparison)	x
Paris/Madrid bombings (comparison)	
Interviews – family/public/neighbours etc	xx

Investigative Framework (TV News Analysis - Newsnight)	
(iv) Social and Cultural Descriptions	
Category	**BBC News - Frequency**
Loyalty	x
Identity	x
British Muslims	xxx
Gender/women	x
Hijab	xx
Muslim/non-Muslim relations	xxxxxxxxxxxx
Christian/Muslim relations	xxx
Government/Muslim relations	x
Conversion	x
Islamophobia	xxx
Racism/Racial tensions	x
Muslim community	xxxxxxxxxxxxx
Segregation/Alienation	xxxx
Deprivation/exclusion/inclusion	xxx
Socio-economic status	x
Attacks on Muslims/backlash/fear	xxxxxxxxx
Mosques	xx
Traditional British values/Assimilation	xxxxx
Hatred	xxxxx
Passport/Citizenship	x

Investigative Framework (TV News Analysis – ITV News) *(v) Politics and Security Issues*	
Category	**BBC News - Frequency**
Fundamentalist/m	
Terrorism/t	xxxxxxxxxx (IF, IT)
Extremism/t	xx
Radical	
Militant	
Dissident	
Insurgency	
Terrorist cells/network	x
Anti-British	
Anti-Western	
Security	x
Threat to national security	
War on terror	
Legislation (anti-terror)	x
Global links/dimension	x
Foreign policy	x
9/11	
Enemy within/outsider implications	
Immigration	
Asylum seekers	
Home Office (visa)	
Names*	xxxxxxx (MSI) xxx (YHO) xxx (RM) xx (OH) xxxx (JCD)
Al-Qaeda	xx
Osama bin Laden	x
Al-Zawahiri	
Omar Bakri Mohamed	
Anjem Chaudry	
Abu Uzair	
Al-Ghuraba	
Groups [Al-Muhajiroun and HT]	
Tony Blair	x
Bomb/bomber	xxxxxxxxxxxxxxxxxxx
Suicide bomb/er	xxxxxxxxx
Anti-terror (Act)	xx
Police (investigation)	xxxxxxxxx
IPCC	
Stop and search (targeting Muslims)	
Murder/conspiracy to murder	
Explosives	
Iraq	xxx
Pakistan	
Saudi Arabia	
Afghanistan	x
Somalia	xxx
Eritrea	x
Kenya	x
Sudan	x
Ethiopia	xx
East Africa	xxx
Northern Ireland (comparison)	
Paris/Madrid bombings (comparison)	xx
Interviews – family/public/neighbours etc	

Investigative Framework (TV News Analysis – ITV News)
(vi) Social and Cultural Descriptions

Category	BBC News - Frequency
Loyalty	
Identity	
British Muslims	
Gender/women	
Hijab	
Muslim/non-Muslim relations	
Christian/Muslim relations	
Government/Muslim relations	
Conversion	
Islamophobia	
Racism/Racial tensions	
Muslim community	
Segregation/Alienation	
Deprivation/exclusion/inclusion	
Socio-economic status	
Attacks on Muslims/backlash/fear	
Mosques	
Traditional British values/Assimilation	
Hatred	
Passport/Citizenship	x

Investigative Framework (TV News Analysis – Channel 4)
(vii) Politics and Security Issues

Category	BBC News - Frequency
Fundamentalist/m	
Terrorism/t	xxxxxxxxxxxxxxxxxxx
Extremism/t	xxxxxxxxxxxxxxxxxxxxxxxx (ME, EP, EC)
Radical Islamic/ist	xxxxxxxx xxx (RF, RC, RIE)
Militant Fanatic	xx x
Dissident	x (SA)
Insurgency	
Terrorist cells	x
Anti-British	
Anti-Western	
Security	
Threat to national security	xxxx
War on terror	
Legislation (anti-terror)	xxx
Global links/dimension	
Foreign policy	xxx
9/11	x
Enemy within/outsider implications	
Immigration Deportation	xxxx
Asylum seekers	xxx
Home Office (visa)	
Names*	xxxxxxx (YHO) xxxxx (MSI) xxxxxxxxx (OH) xx (JCD)
Al-Qaeda	xxxxx
Osama bin Laden	xxx
Al-Zawahiri	xx
Omar Bakri Mohamed	xxxxxxxx
Anjem Chaudry	xx
Abu Uzair	x
Al-Ghuraba	
Groups [Al-Muhajiroun and HT]	xxx (Al-M) xxxxxx (HT)
Tony Blair	xxx
Bomb/bomber	xxxxxxxxxxxxxx
Suicide bomb/er	
Anti-terror (Act)	
Police (investigation)	xxxxxxxxxxxxxxx
IPCC	
Stop and search (targeting Muslims)	
Murder/conspiracy to murder	
Explosives	
Iraq	xxxxx
Pakistan	
Saudi Arabia	xxx
Afghanistan	
Somalia	x
Eritrea	
Kenya	
Sudan	
Ethiopia	
East Africa	
Northern Ireland (comparison)	
Paris/Madrid bombings (comparison)	
Interviews – family/public/neighbours etc	

Investigative Framework (TV News Analysis – Channel 4)
(viii) Social and Cultural Descriptions

Category	BBC News - Frequency
Loyalty	
Identity	
British Muslims	
Gender/women	
Hijab	
Muslim/non-Muslim relations	x
Christian/Muslim relations	
Government/Muslim relations	x
Conversion	
Islamophobia	
Racism/Racial tensions	x
Muslim community	xxxxx
Segregation/Alienation	xxxxxxxx
Deprivation/exclusion/inclusion	xx
Socio-economic status	
Attacks on Muslims/backlash/fear	xx
Mosques	xxxxxxxx
Traditional British values/Assimilation	x
Hatred	
Passport/Citizenship	